THOMAS POINT SHOAL LIGHTHOUSE

THOMAS POINT SHOAL LIGHTHOUSE

A CHESAPEAKE BAY ICON

DAVID GENDELL

The History PRESS

Published by The History Press
Charleston, SC
www.historypress.com

Front cover: Thomas Point Shoal Lighthouse, September 2019. *Photo by David Gendell*. *Back cover*: Major Jared A. Smith took this photograph of the not-yet-ten-year-old Thomas Point Shoal Lighthouse at 6:00 a.m. on August 18, 1885. *National Archives and Records Administration*. *Back cover inset*: The Fourth Order Fresnel lens installed at Thomas Point Shoal Lighthouse in 1899 was removed when the station was automated in 1986, and it is now in safekeeping in the Coast Guard offices at Curtis Bay, near Baltimore. *U.S. Coast Guard*.

First published 2020

Manufactured in the United States

ISBN 9781467145978

Library of Congress Control Number: 2020934339

CONTENTS

Contents

ACKNOWLEDGEMENTS

The Thomas Point Shoal Lighthouse is a beloved centerpiece of the Chesapeake Bay experience. Surprisingly, this is the first book devoted specifically to the lighthouse. Not surprisingly, a number of passionate people stepped forward to contribute to this project.

Over many years, volunteers from the United States Lighthouse Society and its Chesapeake chapter have done groundbreaking work, and they have paved the way for future historians. Their research has provided a solid foundation for all research into Thomas Point history.

In the earliest phase of this project, I purchased several contemporary books devoted to lighthouses, and after reviewing them all, a title published by The History Press stood out. The History Press was the first and only publisher I queried about this project, and it has proven to be an excellent partner. Thank you to the History Press team and acquisition editor Kate Jenkins.

John Potvin opened the doors of the lighthouse, and the time I spent time aboard the screwpile with him and Howard and Cathy Lewis provided valuable content, context and inspiration.

Additional research assistance and access to materials came from Jane Cox, John Yeigh, Sandy Clunies, Tom Cagle and Joe Scanlon. A number of others were helpful and supportive and helped push the project forward and to completion, including Alice Estrada, David Dunigan, Dick Franyo, Terry Hutchinson, Tom Weaver, Mike O'Brien, Lenny Rudow, Mike Burke, Noel Patterson, Bruce Nairn, Debbie Gosselin, Denise Robinson, Camille Gendell and the crew at *SpinSheet* Publishing Company.

I want to include a special recognition for my parents, Mary and Dave Gendell, who had the wherewithal, foresight and energy to load their three young boys on a small sailboat and go cruising on the Chesapeake Bay. It was on one of these expeditions that I first saw the Thomas Point Shoal Lighthouse.

Thank you to Abby Gendell, Delaney Gendell and Trey Gendell, who grew up within earshot of the ship horns at Thomas Point and for the past year have supported me in the creation of this book.

And finally, but never least, thank you to Christine Gendell, who married a guy passionate about this sort of project and who never lost faith in his ability to make it happen.

INTRODUCTION

A lighthouse serves, simultaneously, as a warning and as a guide. A well-placed lighthouse marks shoals and obstacles with a clarity that empowers mariners to navigate safely past. The light of a properly tended lighthouse is dependable and predictable—it penetrates darkness and foul weather and serves as a tangible point of reference through the most challenging conditions. Even modern mariners, sailing with the most advanced satellite navigational systems, recognize and appreciate the presence of a lighthouse. For all mariners—regardless of port of origin, size of ship or cargo carried—a lighthouse is a clearly defined asset on their journey and an aid to navigation.

George Bernard Shaw called lighthouses "altruistic." George Rockwell Putnam, longtime head of the American Lighthouse Service, wrote that the building and keeping of lighthouses represents the "humanitarian work of the nation." "Lighthouses are more helpful than churches," Ben Franklin may or may not have said after narrowly escaping a shipwreck in 1757.

Given their clarity of purpose and benevolent effectiveness, it is no surprise that lighthouses are treasured symbols and structures. The appeal of a lighthouse is universal and apparent both on and off the water.

One particular Chesapeake Bay lighthouse, built in the screwpile style on the deep-water edge of the Thomas Point Shoal, just below Annapolis, has been warning and guiding mariners since 1875. In recent decades, the lighthouse has become a beloved artifact of a simpler time. It is impossible to look at the Thomas Point Shoal Lighthouse and not feel some sense of

Sunrise at the Thomas Point Shoal Lighthouse, October 2019. *Photo by the author.*

warmth and happiness emanating from its history, purpose and physical form. While the structure itself is iconic, the lighthouse at the heart of this book is simultaneously modest and famous, beloved and unlikely, and it is long overdue to have its story broadly told. And yet oddly, the Thomas Point Shoal Lighthouse has always been something of an underdog.

GROUNDINGS ON THE CHESAPEAKE Bay are often more of an inconvenience than a disaster; the Bay bottom is typically soft and the waves relatively mild, and assistance is never too far away. However, any ship grounding disrupts timelines and puts cargo, vessels and mariners at risk. The deep-water channel that connects the busy Baltimore port with the open Atlantic curves and shifts around shoals and obstacles for more than one hundred miles.

Properly marking the hard-packed shoal at Thomas Point had been on the minds of Baltimore's shipping community since at least the early years of the nineteenth century. The shoal, nearly a mile and a half in length and shallow enough for a man to stand on for much of that, pushes boldly out toward the Chesapeake Bay shipping lanes. As early as 1823, Baltimore businessmen were pressing the federal official charged with overseeing the port, demanding an appropriate aid to navigation at Thomas Point. The officer, William Barney, agreed and wrote to his superiors at Washington, D.C.: "Many ship owners and seafaring men of respectability have frequently spoken to me on the subject of a light to be placed at the end of Thomas' Point bar....A light placed here, would be of as great utility as perhaps any one in the Chesapeake Bay."

A lighthouse was soon approved, but it was not placed at the more expensive and challenging location "at the end of Thomas' Point bar" but rather on the point itself, more than one mile from deep water. The first lighthouse on the point, installed in 1825, was a stubby, ineffective stone tower built among trees and on shifting soil. The eroding shoreline at its foundation almost immediately put it at risk of toppling over. Just twenty years after it was initially lit, the tower was taken down and rebuilt nearby on higher ground. Even in its new location, the tower remained a poor aid to navigation. It later fell down, and the land beneath it washed away.

After enduring the stagnant uncertainty of the Civil War, the Port of Baltimore was, by the 1870s, thriving again. With a growing number of foreign and new American ships calling on the port, the path in and out needed to be as clear and straightforward as possible. In the 1870s, the well-organized United States Lighthouse Board began a campaign to mark and light the Chesapeake Bay shoals along the approaches to Baltimore. A new lighthouse on the end of the Thomas Point Shoal, where Barney had initially asked for one to be placed decades earlier, was requested. The U.S. Congress, well aware of Baltimore's crucial role in post–Civil War commerce, approved the request in 1873.

A new lighthouse technology had emerged as a cornerstone of the expanded Chesapeake Bay network: the screwpile. Considered ideal for relatively mild stretches of inland waters, screwpiles could be built less expensively and faster than heavier towers, they required fewer men than lightships and they could be built out over the water, closer to shipping lanes. In an arrangement that would lower costs and increase standardization, sections of the new screwpile cottages were prefabricated ashore, shipped to their final location and then assembled over the water atop a system of iron pilings that had been drilled into the bottom of the Bay.

Not long after their request for funds for a screwpile lighthouse on the Thomas Point Shoal was approved, the engineers of the Lighthouse Board had second thoughts about their chosen design. The screwpile, they had come to realize, was more appropriate for a river or some unworried stretch of water, not the middle of a broad, constantly moving bay. A screwpile built near Thomas Point but in a less exposed position had been severely damaged by ice floes during its first winter. The experts now believed that a fragile screwpile standing at the end of a shoal near the center of the open Chesapeake was a risk too great to bear. They scrambled to ask Congress for additional funding, aiming to build a different, sturdier design at Thomas Point, specifically "a more solid structure, that could be depended upon at all times."

Congress denied the request but made additional funds available to build a stronger version of the screwpile. Through the second half of 1875, the Thomas Point screwpile was rushed to completion before another winter set in. It was the last Chesapeake Bay lighthouse completed that year. The Thomas Point Shoal Lighthouse was first lit in late November 1875, fifty years after it was first requested, and built to a design the experts deemed inappropriate for its location.

NEARLY 150 YEARS LATER, the unlikely screwpile on Thomas Point Shoal still stands and serves, largely due to the efforts of volunteers. The lighthouse on the shoal has also come to represent a healthy public/private partnership that keeps the structure in outstanding condition while staying within documented historic standards. At the same time, even as painting and sanding and repairing goes on all around the structure, the Thomas Point Shoal Lighthouse continues to serve as an active, Coast Guard–managed aid to navigation for mariners and field data station for the National Oceanic and Atmospheric Administration (NOAA).

The core visual aesthetic of the Thomas Point Shoal Lighthouse is simple: it is a slab-sided hexagonal cottage built of wood topped by a light, forty-three feet off the water's surface, all standing on a spindly set of iron piling and braces, with brackish water constantly moving underneath. This cottage is topped by a bright-red metal roof, and the railings on both galleries are trimmed with decorative balusters. In a modern world of glass and steel, beige and gray, the lighthouse at Thomas Point is a crowd-pleasing throwback.

THE THOMAS POINT SHOAL Lighthouse was manned for 111 years. Those who lived aboard and kept the light each had unique experiences at the lighthouse. One keeper scrambled to save equipment as the lighthouse foundation was rocked by drifting ice. Another disappeared mysteriously from the lighthouse and was never seen again. One keeper endured heated interactions with watermen on the shoal, while others witnessed bloodshed related to oyster poaching. One of the station's last keepers ran laps around the lighthouse cottage in an effort to stay in shape, while others played video games to pass the time aboard the lonely station.

This book is not designed to be a comprehensive review of the many keepers of the Thomas Point Shoal Lighthouse, but it does feature a handful of those who served aboard. Others, especially the dedicated historians and researchers with the United States Lighthouse Society and its Chesapeake chapter, have done extraordinary work researching and recognizing the keepers. Over decades, keepers came and went, as do those who serve at the light in the twenty-first century; it is the lighthouse itself that has remained constant. Everyone who has spent time aboard the lighthouse—whether it be to tend the light, service the equipment, sand, paint, clean, repair, tour or guide—feels a shared spirit at Thomas Point. This spirit continues to inspire and motivate the dedicated volunteers who devote time, energy and funds to the lighthouse. According to one of the longest-serving keepers at Thomas Point, time spent aboard the station "gives you time to think about life, yourself, and the purpose for being here on earth."

This book is an earnest effort to shine an overdue light on the point, the shoal, the lighthouse and the associated personalities. The lighthouse structure on the shoal is at the heart of this project, and a portion of the author's proceeds from this book will be donated to Thomas Point Shoal Lighthouse preservation efforts via the United States Lighthouse Society.

This project is designed to be a factual and historically accurate narrative. All dialogue—everything between quotation marks and attributed to a specific person—is derived from original sources: the specific, real-life person actually said or wrote those words and in the context of the topic or scene. A character's unspoken reflections represent a logical re-creation of what was happening at any given time. Similarly, this narrative includes descriptions of scenes and minute-to-minute actions of the subjects, some of which represent logical re-creations of what was happening at any given time. In the instances where any creative license was taken, my research underpinned all my narrative decisions.

This book is dedicated to those who have loved and kept the lighthouse on the shoal—from its brave first keeper, Eugene Burchenal, to the twenty-first-century men and women who volunteer time and donate funds to preserve the structure. It is the author's sincere hope that this book will do a small part in raising awareness of the lighthouse and assist in its preservation for future generations.

THE SHOAL

The shoal at Thomas Point is hard-packed sand and clay, studded with oyster shells. It pushes out toward the center of the Chesapeake Bay at a ninety-degree angle to the shoreline and the current. The shoal is not especially broad, just a few hundred yards at its widest, but it extends out from the shoreline for nearly a mile and a half. For almost all of this length, the water over the shoal is no deeper than seven feet. Across much of the shoal, an average-size adult could stand with his or her head above the surface, even a mile from dry land.

Twice a day, the shoal is washed over with a salty flood tide pushing up the Bay from the Atlantic. And twice a day, the ebb tide drains across the shoal, carrying away the fresher water that pours out of the major rivers to the north. Millennia of flood and ebb have scoured the surface of the shoal—anything soft, easily moved or uncommitted to holding fast is carried away—creating a hard, clean stretch of Bay bottom.

About 7,500 feet offshore, the shoal drops away to deeper water. While mud, sand and clay cannot create the same sharp face of a coral or rock cliff, the drop-off at the end of the shoal is abrupt nonetheless, and the Bay's bottom falls off from eight to forty feet below the surface over the course of about one hundred yards. Just a few miles beyond the end of the shoal is the deepest section of the Chesapeake.

The currents, flood and ebb alike, denied by the shoal of their natural course, endlessly race for the deeper water at its outer edge, where they accelerate to a pace seen nowhere else on this section of the Chesapeake. The shoal bends the tides.

The shoal is immoveable. The shoal is immortal. The shoal is undeniable.

FIRST ENCOUNTERS

Given its location at a narrow part of the Chesapeake Bay and on a fertile peninsula surrounded by water teeming with protein sources, the land now known as Thomas Point was likely a meeting place for indigenous people long before European eyes first sighted it. At the dawn of the seventeenth century, as European colonists struggled for an initial foothold in North America, several major Native American kingdoms thrived in lands adjacent to Thomas Point: the Susquehannocks to the north, the Powhatans to the south and the Nanticokes to the east, across the Chesapeake Bay. The peninsula itself was located on the edges of each of these expansive kingdoms. It is reasonable to assume that the centrally located peninsula was the site of gatherings, hunting and fishing expeditions and stopovers on passages up and down the Bay.

The legacy of the Native American presence was found in the peninsula's soil by twentieth-century researchers in the form of shards of Rappahannock fabric-impressed pottery and a full-grooved axe. It is likely that nineteenth-century digging at the now-vanished section of the peninsula—including that which took place in the building of the initial stone lighthouse towers—yielded considerably more artifacts. Even without digging, additional evidence of a meaningful Native American presence on the peninsula was visible to the initial European visitors, the men who later built and kept the stone towers at the point, and well into the twentieth century: piles of oyster shells.

The region's indigenous people relied on the Chesapeake Bay for sustenance. For centuries, oysters—plentiful, packed with protein and relatively easy to harvest—were a component of the regional diet. As Native Americans harvested and consumed oysters, their shells were piled into holes and stacked in heaps, creating shell middens. In 1971, a Late Woodland Period oyster shell midden was recorded at the Thomas Point peninsula. This midden, located on a narrow section of the point, about one thousand yards from the location of the first lighthouse tower, was named "Marshy Point" and dated to AD 950–1600. At that time, the midden extended nearly one hundred yards along the shoreline, pushed nearly forty feet inland and was more than one foot deep. In 1971, quantities of shell could be seen (without digging) in the water, along the shoreline and in an embankment. The area was eroding rapidly, and in the spring of 1977, a bulkhead was constructed in the area of the midden, completely destroying it. It is noteworthy to recognize that the Thomas Point shell midden predated the stone towers on the point by centuries and survived them by many decades.

As the Native Americans fished, hunted and lived at the land on and near Thomas Point, the first Europeans began visiting the area. Shadowy legends exist of sixteenth-century Spanish explorers on the lower Chesapeake Bay. These early visitors may have ventured as far north as Thomas Point in undocumented but not unlikely explorations. One doomed Spanish expedition carried Jesuit priests and made landfall on a Chesapeake Bay shoreline nearly forty years before Jamestown was settled. The priests aimed to establish a mission along the rivers of Virginia's western shore, but Powhatan natives cut the effort short, killing the priests. A Spanish supply ship arrived shortly afterward and was approached by men in canoes dressed as clerics. The Spanish sailors, better prepared for hostilities than the unarmed priests, were able to kill several of the native attackers but soon abandoned plans for settlement in the region. The memory of these bloody exchanges lingered when the English Jamestown expedition arrived in the lower Chesapeake in 1607.

Among the Jamestown expedition was the fiery John Smith, who was charged with mutiny and under arrest for most of the transatlantic passage. Once North America was reached, he emerged as a strong leader. Conditions at the Jamestown settlement were brutal: food was difficult to source, relations with the natives was strained and often violent and more than half of the original settlers died. With this backdrop, Smith twice sailed north into the Chesapeake Bay in an effort to further explore the region. While mapping the region, claiming land for the British empire and establishing trading posts were practical goals, Smith and his crew were also motivated by loftier dreams and, in the pursuit of them, would be disappointed by the Chesapeake. It was hoped that explorations into the North American continent would produce material treasures, including gold and silver. All the while, perhaps a new route to the Pacific could be discovered up any river or bay. As they slowly moved up the Chesapeake in the summer heat, Smith and the sailors in a modest, open boat knew that finding the fabled passage would be a life-changing event. It was not to be.

On the first of these voyages, in June 1608, Captain John Smith and his small crew hugged the western shore of the Bay and along the way were likely the first Europeans to see what is now known as Thomas Point. In the vicinity of Thomas Point, Smith made the following entry in his exploration journal:

> [T]*he Westerne shore by which we sayled we found all along well watered, but very mountanous and barren, the vallies very fertill, but extreame thicke of small wood so well as trees, and much frequented with Wolves, Beares, Deere and other wild beasts.*

In the text accompanying the 1612 map he made of the area, John Smith indicated his strong feelings for the region, despite the lack of gold or a Pacific passage: "The situation of the rivers are so propitious to the nature and use of man as no place is more convenient for pleasure, profit and man's sustenance."

By 1627, William Claiborne, a successful and enterprising Virginia colonist, was conducting a thriving fur trade business up and down the Chesapeake. Backed by a syndicate of London merchants and holding a royal trading commission permitting him to trade with natives in any area of the Mid-Atlantic where similar agreements were not already in effect, Claiborne aimed to set up a trading post on an island directly across the Chesapeake from Thomas Point and roughly midway between his operations on the Susquehanna River and in the Virginia colony. Claiborne named the island Kent after his native home in England. In the spring of 1631 at Kent Island, Claiborne opened a trading post, built a fort and a private residence and soon attracted more than one hundred settlers. In establishing his settlement, Claiborne had declared his allegiance to the colony of Virginia rather than Maryland, the colony that completely enveloped Kent Island and whose new capital, Annapolis, would soon be established within view of Kent Island. Thus began a lengthy dispute between Virginia and Maryland. By 1658, Claiborne had been forcefully removed from the island and returned to Virginia.

Virginia's claim on the island, however, was not officially settled for more than one hundred years.

In 1650, as Claiborne's settlement and associated dispute grew on the Eastern Shore, Europeans began to explore and settle the western shore around present-day Annapolis. Among the earliest Europeans to settle the area was Philip Thomas, who came to Maryland in 1651 from Bristol, England, with his wife and three daughters. The well-connected Thomas assembled several tracts of land, including, in 1665, 120 acres on the peninsula between the Severn and South Rivers, a section of which was called Fuller's Point and was subsequently named Thomas's Point. Thomas received this stretch of waterfront land as part of a grant from Cecil Calvert, the Right Honorable Second Lord Baltimore, who managed his extensive American holdings from his estate in North Yorkshire, England. Cecil Calvert never visited Maryland. Anne Arundel County is named for his wife.

There are indications that Philip Thomas attempted to establish a ferry from the point to the Eastern Shore, but no record exists of this as anything more than a concept. No lasting structures or infrastructure were built on the peninsula in Thomas's lifetime. Philip Thomas died in 1675 and is buried at the Quaker Burying Ground in Galesville, Maryland. His heirs sold the property in 1705, and it changed hands several times over the years.

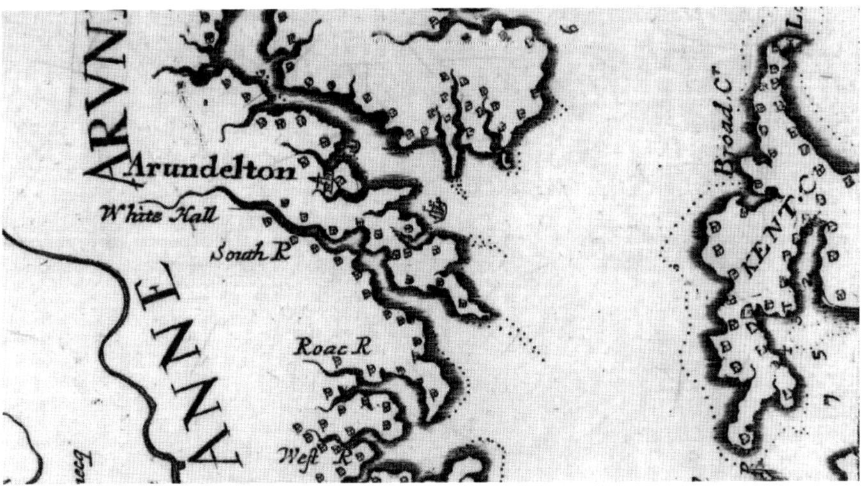

Detail of a map Augustine Herman completed in 1670 for Cecil Calvert, the Second Lord Baltimore. In exchange for the map, Calvert granted Herman large tracts of land in the northern Chesapeake region. At the same time Herman was producing the map, Calvert made a land grant to Philip Thomas that included the land now known as Thomas Point. This map shows the Thomas Point Shoal, extending into the Chesapeake from the northern side of the mouth of the South River. *Library of Congress.*

By the turn of the nineteenth century, the peninsula was owned by Jeremiah Townley Chase, a well-connected, high-achieving Annapolitan. Chase represented Maryland at the Continental Congress in 1783 and 1784 while serving as mayor of Annapolis. As mayor, Chase officially welcomed General George Washington to Annapolis on the occasion of his resigning his military commission. Chase later served as a justice on Maryland's General Court. In 1806, Chase was appointed chief justice of the Maryland Court of Appeals and served in that role through his retirement in 1826. Along the way, Chase speculated in land, focusing on property owned by former Tories in and around Annapolis and at Baltimore. His political connections, access to legal proceedings and information and the anti-Tory sentiment among the population doubtlessly aided this pursuit. The land at Thomas Point came into the property portfolio of Jeremiah Chase. The peninsula boasted no meaningful buildings or settlements, but it was heavily wooded, easily accessed from Annapolis and featured a lengthy stretch of coastline, making it ideal for hunting parties, especially those focused on waterfowl. Chase and his friends doubtlessly hunted the land, but so did others. Frustrated with unauthorized visitors on his land, Chase placed a series of advertisements in the Annapolis newspapers warning that "the law will be put in force" against anyone hunting or trespassing on his Thomas Point property.

In the spring of 1813, just a few miles from the chief justice's Annapolis home, the Royal Navy invaded and occupied Maryland's Chesapeake Bay. Thomas Point, and its high-profile owner, had a front-row view of the action.

WAR ARRIVES AT THE SHOAL

Thomas Point, Annapolis, Maryland
Spring of 1813

Maryland governor Levin Winder allowed himself a private smile as he squinted out across the shallow water. Less than an hour earlier, he had been roused from his desk and hurried to a fast horse in order to bear witness to the odd scene now before him and, presumably, pass judgment on it. On the harried ride out to the point, he had been briefed on what to expect, but now, on the water's edge, he found himself unable to turn away. A nearby aide offered a viewing scope, but the governor brushed it away. His own eyes were enough. The situation before him would soon require him to make a hard decision that would lead, inevitably, into controversy; at first encounter, though, there *was* some element of humor to it.

The Bay spread before him swelled brackish and alive through the center of his state, and it had been invaded. In the distance to the south, he saw the unmistakable shape of two large enemy warships under sail. Across the narrow Bay, he spotted a smaller warship against the dark, wooded profile of the Eastern Shore. To his endless frustration, the governor had no idea *how many* enemy ships floated in his state. The estimated number seemed to grow with every report, as did the tension among the citizens. Now, one of these dreaded ships had revealed itself in the afternoon sunlight, a few hundred yards off the shoreline and just a few miles away from his official residence.

This particular enemy ship was, however, not actually *floating* on the Bay; rather, it was aground on the shoal that extends into the Bay off the rural peninsula known as Thomas Point.

It was the contrast between the ongoing threat of the enemy fleet and the immediate helplessness of this ship before him that led to the private smile. *If we don't have the firepower to defeat the fleet, perhaps our shoals will do the job and stop them one by one.* The governor's glib thought and his smile didn't last long. The war with England was no longer a concept, no longer a report in a newspaper and no longer the smudge of distant ships on the horizon. Governor Winder could now find the war a quick ride south and east of his state's capitol building. The war was now visible in the form of a British Royal Navy sloop bouncing in the light chop off the hard clay of the Thomas Point Shoal with a *thud-thud-thud* that shook its rigging and could be heard by the governor and the small party of men that had gathered with him on the point to investigate.

The tide is still falling, the men reminded the governor, multiple times—in his office, on the ride out from Annapolis and now, again, at the point. A light but steady southerly wind continued to push the sloop toward ever-more shallow water. Before the governor and his party arrived on the point, the sloop's crew lowered its sails to slow the progress into shallower water. But still, each small wave lifted the wooden hull a few inches off the shoal, and the wind and waves then pushed it a short but agonizing step farther into the shallows before it landed with the *thud* and started the process again. The sloop's crew scrambled across the deck in animated conversation, presumably trying to set an anchor. The governor noted that the crew of a sloop aground on a falling tide, on a lee shore and nearly within hailing distance of the American shoreline, moved with real urgency. He also noted a distress flag that had been run up and now flapped lazily in the soft breeze.

Governor Levin Winder was not a seafaring man, but even he could see, without the glass, that this sloop was in no immediate danger of breaking up. The thudding in the small waves was more of an annoyance than a death knell. This was all an embarrassment more than anything. If allowed to run their natural course, the tide and wind would eventually turn or assistance would arrive and the sloop would float freely, able to convey its master to what would certainly be a difficult conversation with Admiral George Cockburn aboard his flagship.

The governor *was* a military man, however, and he could see that the grounded enemy ship *was* well within reach of a cannon firing from the point. The animated conversation around him revealed this option to be strongly appealing to most of the men assembled at the point with him.

As his men discussed the logistics of a cannon assault, the governor looked to the north, where two American schooners sliced away toward Baltimore, their sleek profiles more distant by the minute. He surmised that this pair had been under pursuit by the British sloop and that they had lured it toward the shoal at Thomas Point. Once on the shoal, the American pair skirted across safely, mere inches of water under their own keels, while the invaders thudded to a sudden halt in the shallows. The point itself was named and its shoal visible on the charts the British carried aboard their ships, but a wartime engagement with crafty American sailors could lead an overheated British captain to ignore his chart. *The Baltimore ships were fast and their crews enterprising*, the governor thought. Admiral George Cockburn, the lead of the British invasion of the Chesapeake, had made no secret that Baltimore was a desirable target. This grounding incident would only stoke that desire.

As Levin Winder watched the Baltimore schooners move farther north, the governor imagined the American sailors enjoying a few minutes of laughter as they recounted the sharp end of the pursuit. He knew that the American sailors' retelling of their heroic story, unpacked to rapt audiences within the salty pubs of Baltimore's Fells Point district, would expand. In these versions, the unlucky sloop in pursuit of the Americans might have been a massive frigate or perhaps even George Cockburn's own flagship. Perhaps, a version might hold, the Americans lured the invaders to a watery grave. Or perhaps some might boast that as the Patriot schooners sailed safely away, their crews looked aft and saw the Annapolis locals moving off the point toward the grounded ship—swarming over and through the shallow water—and claiming it in the name of free trade and the United States. The true story of the grounding, so far, was far less dramatic.

One of the sloop's crew had entered the chilly water and stood on the shoal with the Bay up to his chin. The governor tried to ignore the animated conversation swirling around him on the point and held his gaze seaward for another moment, watching as the overboard sailor's shipmates handed down a small anchor that the sailor would soon walk or swim out away from the sloop and attempt to secure in deeper water. After another quick, private smile, Governor Winder turned to engage his traveling party that, by this point, was fervently intent on attacking and destroying the stranded vessel as quickly as possible. The governor took one last look at the stranded sloop and thought, *This is going to be an uncomfortable but important couple of hours.*

ALTHOUGH HE HAD AN impressive record as a Revolutionary War officer, Levin Winder was elected governor of Maryland on a crest of antiwar sentiment. A few months before his election, the U.S. Congress, at the urging of President James Madison, had declared war on Great Britain, citing numerous grievances against the empire, most of them involving its powerful Royal Navy. The Congressional vote for war was split along party lines, with Madison and his fellow Republicans carrying the day.

Despite his personal opposition to the war, and the strident antiwar sentiment of his own Federalist Party, Levin Winder took office knowing that the war was inevitably coming and that an aggressive defense of his state would be necessary. The Chesapeake Bay was a primary focus of the Royal Navy; Maryland's ports and commerce presented alluring targets. Governor Winder knew that owing to the heated political rivalries of the moment, securing needed assistance from the federal government would be difficult.

The Eastern Shore native and veteran politician began his first one-year term in November 1812 and immediately began writing to Washington officials in search of additional support; the British approach was all but inevitable. His pleas were largely ignored. Winder pointed out that Maryland's waterways provided a direct route to the nation's capital and that little resistance was in place. The state's lightly defended capital, Annapolis, was a largely symbolic prize for the British—it had been a hub of Revolutionary activity—and could easily be accessed by the British fleet now gathering in the Chesapeake Bay. Baltimore, the state's largest city, was also an attractive target. Its ships and sailors had been delivering havoc to British trade in all corners of the Atlantic and into the Mediterranean. A sharp British strike into Baltimore's shipbuilding hub would give the invaders an emotional jolt and practical triumph. With no answers from Washington, Winder knew that Maryland would need to coalesce and defend itself.

By the spring of 1813, the Chesapeake Bay had been blockaded by the British Royal Navy, and every settlement along Maryland's shoreline was living under the threat of imminent invasion. The hated British admiral George Cockburn and his fleet cruised the length of the waterway threatening disruption and destruction. The only impediments slowing the British in the Chesapeake seemed to be a lack of food to fuel the several thousand sailors operating in the region—a problem solved by farm raids that only served to increase the intense anti-British sentiment in the area—and the fleet's frequent groundings in the Bay's soft bottom, a problem less easily solved.

George Cockburn's early dispatches to his commanding officer, Admiral Sir John B. Warren, are filled with mentions of groundings and their consequences. In mid-April 1813, he wrote from Swan Creek, near Rock Hall, Maryland, "I am endeavoring to have the position of the different Shoals and Knowles around us ascertained and buoyed off." Despite the annoying reality of "Shoals and Knowles" and the need to assign men and resources to charting them, Cockburn's menacing presence was seen and felt along the Maryland waterfront. Resistance would be met by destruction.

Cockburn sprang into action in the first days of May at Havre de Grace, a sleepy northern Bay town. The town's name had been inspired by a comment from the hated Lafayette, and this perhaps raised the emotional stakes for the British sailors. Cockburn later admitted, however, that it was the sight of an American flag flying over a freshly constructed battery that inspired his fierce attack. In a sharp attack, the town's battery was captured, forty of the town's sixty houses were burned and cannons were removed. Only one American died in the raid, but Cockburn's reputation grew immensely, as did the tensions on and along the Chesapeake. News of British raids quickly spread along the waterfront.

Inflicting damage at the major American port of Baltimore was a British goal, as was an invasion of Washington, D.C., but many Annapolis residents remained convinced that their city was also a highly desirable target for an attack. Annapolitans could see British ships moving up and down the Bay from their town docks. When British ships appeared at the mouth of the Severn River and began taking soundings in an effort to record and mark the "Shoals and Knowles," some Annapolis residents packed valuables and fled the city.

Governor Winder appealed directly to President James Madison and again was ignored. Maryland was, at the time, a Federalist state with a Federalist governor. Madison, a Republican, would not budge for Maryland, although he provided federal assistance to nearby states, including Republican Virginia. In response, Winder remarked, "Virginia has but to ask and she receives; but Maryland, for her political disobedience, is denied." Winder considered moving the state's official records to a safer, inland location. He prepared to call a special session of the state legislature to discuss even more drastic actions, including calling the state militia into Baltimore and Annapolis. He prepared for a large-scale invasion.

It was against this stark backdrop that a breathless pair of men burst into the governor's office and reported a British warship, unaccompanied and aground, on the shoal at Thomas Point.

THE MEN AT THE point agreed that the grounded sloop could be reached by a well-placed cannon. But the sloop was already on the bottom and could not be sunk further. It was then proposed that heated cannon shot would catch the wooden sloop on fire and burn it to the waterline, destroying the hull and sending its crew onto the shoal.

The governor agreed that heated shot, launched from the point, could destroy the sloop. He also knew that the land from which they would be firing that heated shot, Thomas Point, was owned by Jeremiah Chase, a former mayor of Annapolis, a member of the Continental Congress and, at this time, chief justice on the State Board of Appeals. Surely, Levin Winder thought to himself, Jeremiah Chase would want to weigh in on any attack launched from his land.

Winder, wary of the formidable Chase but likely more concerned about making Annapolis a more attractive target for the British fleet, listened to the proposals but steadfastly delayed any action. The lobbying continued, with the majority of the party in favor of bold action. Winder stayed cool-headed in his spoiler role. Any aggressive action, he explained, would only further antagonize Cockburn and fuel their aggression against his state's ill-prepared, undermanned defenses. His aides and companions pressed forward.

The prize can be easily plucked.

There are no cannons at this position, Winder countered.

Cannons can be moved to the point from Annapolis.

The point has no defenses, and should the British move against it, they could march straight into Annapolis over land.

Order men to the point, and earthen breastworks can be built up very quickly.

There is no facility at the point to heat the shot.

A nearby log-house can be converted to a heating operation.

As the discussion took place ashore, several British ships rushed to the grounded sloop and were soon hove-to in the deep water just off the shoal, alert and ready with gun ports open and bayonets glinting in the late afternoon sun. *Statira*, a powerful thirty-eight-gun frigate capable of inflicting great damage on lightly defended Annapolis, was soon among the rescuers. Governor Winder pointed out the assembling fleet and flatly refused to order any sort of attack on the sloop.

As evening approached, the group returned to Annapolis, discussing *what-ifs* and *if-onlys* behind the governor's back in the spring twilight.

British Fifth-Rate Frigate HMS *Menelaus* (*center*), a sistership of *Statira*. *Menelaus* also operated in the upper Chesapeake during the War of 1812. *National Maritime Museum, Greenwich, London.*

GOVERNOR WINDER'S DECISION PROVED controversial and was analyzed on Annapolis docks and in the town's pubs for days. He had allowed a vulnerable British prize to escape unmolested, and for many citizens, this outrage was compounded by the arriving news of Cockburn's aggression at Havre de Grace.

Accounts of the Havre de Grace destruction ran in newspapers alongside fiery editorials and letters supporting or denouncing Winder's decision out at Thomas Point. Had the destruction of the ship been allowed to take place, an article in the *Maryland Gazette* declared, "the triumph would have been glorious for us." However, the *Gazette* ultimately proclaimed that the governor "is a man of such military experience and sound judgement that we believe his decision may be safely confided in, notwithstanding the assertions of his traducers to the contrary."

Unsurprisingly, the *Maryland Republican*, a voice of Winder's rival political party, was fierce in its condemnation of Winder and his decision. The newspaper pledged an investigation and declared that when the facts were disclosed, the governor "shall be exposed and stigmatized as a Tory and a traitor to his country."

While the debate raged in Annapolis, tide and wind aligned out at the point, and a well-handled British ship ventured close to the shoal. With the assistance of a longboat, cables were passed across to the stranded sloop, and the process of freeing it from the shoal began.

Several days after the grounding, the *Maryland Republican* published a report accusing Levin Winder of saying he was "glad" to hear that the sloop had been freed. The alleged comment set off another firestorm of controversy. Governor Winder took to the press himself, writing a letter that called the accusation against him "False, base and infamous." The debate began over who made the charge against Winder, and the repercussions filled columns upon columns of broadsheets. Nonetheless, Winder was reelected to two more terms as Maryland's governor and is remembered as a unifying, steady force during the British invasion and occupation of his state.

Admiral George Cockburn, who lit fires and tasted destruction at Havre de Grace and later played a key role in the sacking of Washington, D.C., was well informed of how the situation at Thomas Point unfolded and well aware of Levin Winder's decision. Years later, according to legend, Admiral George Cockburn encountered an Annapolis gentleman. After the incident at the shoal was recounted, the admiral congratulated the Annapolis man on the prudence shown by the town's citizens and its leaders. Cockburn then declared that had even a single gun been fired toward the grounded ship, he would have sacked Annapolis in half an hour.

BALTIMORE RISING

Nothing indicates the liberality, prosperity, or intelligence of a nation more clearly than the facilities which it affords for the safe approach of the mariner to its shores.
—Report of the Lighthouse Board to the United States Congress, November 6, 1868

While the Thomas Point Shoal Lighthouse is now inextricably linked with the city of Annapolis—the city, in fact, is the present owner of the structure—the story of its creation and the very reasons for its existence are, unequivocally, connected with Baltimore.

The Chesapeake Bay pushes into the heart of a fertile, industrious region of North America, and in natural course, ports of various sizes and states of organization developed along its shores. Jamestown, Virginia, England's first colonial port in North America, is about forty miles up the James River from the Chesapeake and about sixty miles from the open Atlantic. Building port facilities at this location was among the first projects undertaken by the initial settlers. In short order, other ports and trading posts opened and expanded along the Bay, including those in Virginia at Hampton, Norfolk, Portsmouth and Suffolk. In Maryland, on the northern portion of the Bay, port and trading facilities opened and thrived at Oxford, Cambridge, Crisfield, Rock Hall and Annapolis.

Throughout the first half of the eighteenth century, Maryland's capital, Annapolis, emerged as one of colonial America's most developed and attractive cities, although its port was relatively shallow and compact. The port had been designated as an official port of entry by British authorities, and as the neighboring colonies grew, Annapolis became a busy stopover for travelers. Its location on the edge of a relatively narrow section of the Chesapeake made it an ideal terminus for a ferry crossing to Maryland's Eastern Shore. At Annapolis, travelers moving north and south along the Atlantic Seaboard could easily find a boat to take them across the Bay, shaving miles off their route. A swirl of entertainment and activity was available in Annapolis to keep travelers occupied as they awaited departure.

As the colonial population grew, and then after the United States of America was established, demands for the region's grain, tobacco and, later, coal also expanded. Settlements along the Mid-Atlantic's Fall Line, where the coastal plain met the Piedmont Plateau, grew rapidly in both population and importance. These settlements were established at the upper reaches of navigable water, typically just below first falls and rapids encountered when traveling upstream. They were much farther inland than the Chesapeake's coastal ports and, as a result, enjoyed greater proximity to the fertile farmland and coal deposits of the interior. Among the region's Fall Line ports are the Virginia cities of Petersburg, Richmond, Fredericksburg and Alexandria; Philadelphia to the north, in Pennsylvania; and Baltimore, in Maryland. Not coincidentally, these ports were aligned with the Mid-Atlantic's major north–south travel artery and today lie roughly along the path of Interstate 95.

Among these Fall Line ports, Baltimore especially thrived. The city's proximity to extensive uplands allowed inland producers to move harvests and products downstream to tidal waters with relative ease. The mechanics involved in turning grain into flour via a series of mills and machinery could be powered by naturally moving water, which ran a short distance from the saltwater port. From the docks at Baltimore, the broad world opened as a market. An extensive shoreline, served by deep water, allowed for expansion. With these pieces in place, the catalyst for Baltimore's successful recipe were the city's business and municipal leaders, who began an effort to develop and maintain a position as a welcoming international port that continues to this day.

In 1780, Baltimore was recognized as an official port of entry, and its eclipse of Annapolis, which lacked many of the key elements required of an international shipping center, became inevitable. After this official designation and the subsequent expansion of facilities, Baltimore's population expanded fifteenfold between 1790 and 1860, while Annapolis's barely doubled in the same period. At the same time, Baltimore's fortifications expanded and solidified, while Annapolis's were abandoned. So complete was Baltimore's rise that in 1813 and 1814, when the invading British raided the settlements along the Chesapeake Bay, they largely ignored Annapolis, while applying great focus to plans for the destruction of shipbuilding and commercial enterprises along Baltimore's waterfront.

By 1830, Baltimore was the second-most populated city in the United States. The city held the position for the next three decades.

Underpinning the commercial growth were generations of Baltimore business leaders who relentlessly innovated and invested in the port's connections with the growing production and productivity of America's Midwest. In early 1827, a group of Baltimore businessmen created the Baltimore and Ohio Railroad Company and began expanding the rail network into the heartland. Over the next fifty years, the line grew and eventually formed a critical connection with Chicago, 811 miles distant. Another rail line connected Baltimore with Wilmington, Philadelphia and points north. The Annapolis port—shallow, lacking moving water and located on a peninsula 30 miles east of the Fall Line transport routes—could not compete.

Coal, lumber, cotton goods, cattle and other bulky, expensive-to-ship cargos were delivered by rail and road to Baltimore and loaded onto vessels that then moved them out to the world, efficiently and inexpensively. For much of the nineteenth century, Baltimore's ascent was propelled by an outbound flow of grain, grown in the broad fields of Northern Virginia, Western Maryland and Pennsylvania, often ground into fine flour before loading onto ships and much in demand in Europe and South America.

From the Ocean to Baltimore

About 150 miles of Chesapeake Bay lie between the open ocean and Baltimore's piers. As the city grew in importance, so did the need to safely move ships and cargos across this distance. As a ship moves north up the Bay, toward Baltimore, the shorelines close in, and shoals lie closer to the shipping lanes. While a grounding on the Chesapeake is typically not catastrophic—the Bay's bottom is typically soft and a flood tide can free most grounded vessels—a grounding could cause costly delays in shipping schedules, spoil a perishable cargo and, in extreme cases, damage a ship's rudder or propellers.

Since 1852, the State of Maryland has sanctioned an association of professional pilots who use thorough understanding of the Bay's geography both above and below the waterline to safely guide large ships transiting up and down the Chesapeake. The creation of the association unified and structured a number of independent pilot groups that had been operating on the Bay since the nineteenth century. However, even accredited Bay pilots reference landmarks and charts as they transit the Chesapeake, especially at night and in foul weather, and not every ship carries a pilot. As Baltimore expanded, it became clear that a well-understood, well-maintained, evergreen system of navigational aids was needed to ensure safe passages and the steady flow of shipborne commerce. As a result, the first federally funded lighthouse on the Chesapeake Bay was lit in 1822—a simple stone tower at the mouth of the final shipping approach to Baltimore. Dozens more of them would follow.

Most interested in the safe passage of ships to and from the port were the owners and managers of the shipping concerns that lined the wharves at Baltimore. The city's shipping industry provided thousands of jobs and generated a steady flow of custom fees and taxes for local, state and federal governments. Collectively, this group could produce a strong lobby at the statehouse at Annapolis and, when necessary, could even influence decisions in Washington. Looking for a single point of contact to manage the situation, the federal government placed an official at the port and charged him with overseeing federal interests, prioritizing projects and managing communications with Washington. Through the heady expansion of the 1820s, the naval officer for the Port of Baltimore was William Bedford Barney, a well-known hero of the War of 1812 with a long family history in Maryland and a family name that made early Americans swell with pride.

WILLIAM BEDFORD BARNEY

In May 1781, twenty-two-year-old American naval officer Joshua Barney entered his fifth month as a war prisoner behind the stone walls at the Old Mill Prison at Plymouth, England. Frustrated, starved for information about the war and prone to bold action, Barney made an escape attempt and was promptly caught. As punishment, he spent thirty days in solitary confinement, bound in heavy irons. Undeterred, Barney almost immediately began plotting another attempt. This plan was more elaborate and ultimately effective. After dressing as a British officer and scaling a twenty-five-foot-high wall, the Maryland native found freedom and, in the process, wrote the first chapter of a new American legend. Upon returning home to Baltimore, Joshua Barney married Anne Bedford, and by the end of 1781, Anne had given birth to a son: William Bedford Barney. It seems unfair, two centuries later, to intertwine a father's story with his son's, but the Barneys are inextricably linked and forever connected with Thomas Point and the young United States.

William Barney's boyhood unfolded in a hotbed of patriotism and adventure. His father was often away at sea serving in high-profile roles for the American and French causes. With transatlantic tensions constantly simmering and the ongoing legend of his father influencing his every move, it was only natural that young William Barney follow his father into service.

Father and son served together in the War of 1812 and participated in heated action while defending the shores of the Chesapeake Bay. William Barney's bravery is noted in records of those conflicts, and he became an early United States marine. In June 1814, at the Battle of St. Leonard Creek off the Patuxent River, about forty miles south of Annapolis, the thirty-two-year-old William Barney boarded a flaming American gun barge that had been hit by a British rocket. With his father and hundreds of others looking on, he single-handedly extinguished the fire and saved the barge. In September 1814, William Barney led the Maryland Dragoons in the intense Battle of North Point; it took place just east of Baltimore, on Barney family land.

After the war, President James Monroe placed William Barney in a diplomatic post at Trieste, Italy, and, after about two years of European service, Monroe brought him home. Back in the United States, Barney married the well-connected Mary Chase, the daughter of Judge Samuel Chase, who had signed the Declaration of Independence and served as an associate justice of the United States Supreme Court, appointed to the position by President George Washington. By October 1817, the couple had five young children, with many more to come.

After his heroic service in the War of 1812, William Barney's legendary father, Commodore Joshua Barney, was named naval officer for the Port of Baltimore. As the lead federal representative at Baltimore, Joshua Barney was involved in all aspects of the port, including customs operations, port defenses and ongoing liaisons with the city's commercial seafaring community. After a few years in the high-profile role, Commodore Barney's health began to fail, and he was keen to retire inland. In response, in 1818,

President Monroe appointed Commodore Barney's son, William Barney, to the position. Later that year, Joshua Barney died from the effects of earlier battle wounds.

The naval officer in charge of the port at Baltimore was a plum but busy role. This position allowed the Barney family to establish a permanent residence in Baltimore, where they took an active place in the city's society and raised their family, which eventually grew to include twelve children.

In 1820, Stephen Pleasonton, a well-connected Washington civil servant with no real maritime experience, took charge of the nascent American lighthouse network and almost immediately began aggressively delegating responsibilities to local officials at harbors across the United States. As Pleasonton pushed tasks his way, William Barney's role expanded. He stayed in constant contact with shipping company officers, ship captains and others in the industry. Given Baltimore's location and its importance in national commerce, the challenges of transiting the Chesapeake Bay were a regular topic. As port projects were debated and proposed, William Barney quickly learned that Stephen Pleasonton was a budget hawk.

STEPHEN PLEASONTON

As a career Washington civil servant, Stephen Pleasonton's primary role in the American story was defined well before he connected with lighthouses. Pleasonton was working at Washington as a senior clerk in the U.S. State Department in 1814 when news arrived of an imminent British invasion; George Cockburn and company were on the verge of reaching their ultimate goal. As the British approached, President James Madison ordered Pleasonton to remove important books and papers housed at the State Department. The clerk famously gathered records and artifacts into coarse linen bags for transport to safety outside of the city.

Among the documents Pleasonton collected were George Washington's commission and correspondence, as well as the original copies of the Constitution and the Articles of Confederation. According to legend, as Pleasonton prepared to depart with the bags, he noticed the original Declaration of Independence hanging on the wall in a frame and collected it as well. As Pleasonton carried the rescued cache west of Washington via wagon, the British arrived and burned many government buildings. Stephen

The often-controversial Stephen Pleasonton, who oversaw the United States Lighthouse system from 1820 through 1852. During Pleasonton's tenure, the first lighthouse tower was constructed at Thomas Point and then rebuilt fifteen years later. *U.S. National Archives and Records Administration.*

Pleasonton quickly gained recognition as the man who dramatically saved treasured records of the early United States.

In 1817, the nation's capital returned to postwar normalcy, and President James Monroe appointed Pleasonton to a senior role at the Treasury Department. As "Fifth Auditor," Pleasonton was given responsibility for a broad scope of the Treasury Department's business with the State Department and Patent Office. Although he had no maritime experience, responsibility for overseeing all the aids to navigation in the United States was moved into Pleasonton's portfolio in 1820. Stephen Pleasonton stayed in command of the American lighthouse network for the next thirty-two years.

Stephen Pleasonton's lengthy tenure coincides with the pressing need for expansion of the lighthouse network, and it was expanded under his watch. Unfortunately, his tenure was also defined by penny-pinching, Congressional investigations and a high degree of delegation. Pleasonton's legacy with the American lighthouse network is typically harshly judged by historians.

Frequently cited as an example of the negative consequences of Pleasonton's leadership is an 1825 incident off North Carolina's Outer

Banks. The important lightship at Diamond Shoals was blown off its station by a strong winter storm, and in the process, its anchor chain snapped, leaving the anchor and a lengthy section of chain on the bottom. The lightship limped to Norfolk, and the news was immediately sent north to Washington, D.C. Pleasonton's response was to offer a $500 reward for salvage of the anchor and chain; together they were worth about $2,000. Pleasonton eventually relented, but the lightship had remained off-station for months, putting mariners in real danger and confounding insurance and shipping executives.

Even as the need for more lighthouses, updated equipment and proper training grew, so did the unpleasant reputation of Stephen Pleasonton.

THE SITUATION AT THE THOMAS POINT SHOAL

Among the troublesome obstacles in the final stretch of the inbound voyage to Baltimore is Thomas Point Shoal. About twenty miles southeast of the final approach to Baltimore Harbor, the shoal reaches out more than one mile toward the center of the Chesapeake, carrying water depths of just six or seven feet its entire length. By 1823, the shoal at Thomas Point had become enough of a concern in the shipping offices at Baltimore that William Barney contacted Stephen Pleasonton and asked for a new lighthouse to mark the obstacle. On December 22, 1823, William Barney wrote:

> *Many ship owners and seafaring men of respectability have frequently spoken to me on the subject of a light to be placed at the end of Thomas' Point bar, a few miles below Annapolis; which extends a considerable distance out into the Bay, cutting the direct track of vessels bound up or down; at the end of which from four feet, you instantly deepen to six and seven fathoms water. A light placed here, would be of as great utility as perhaps any one in the Chesapeake Bay.*

It is meaningful that Barney specifically referenced a light "placed at the end of Thomas' Point bar." Given the expense and complications of establishing a meaningful light in the middle of the Chesapeake Bay, Pleasonton's response was predictable. He appreciated the need to mark the shoal, but what the ship owners, the seafaring men of respectability and the naval officer for the Port of Baltimore asked for is not what they received. Rather than a light at the end of the shoal, Pleasonton offered up a tower on shore, a simpler and less expensive alternative, and at his request, Congress approved the shore tower plan and appropriated $6,500 toward it on May 26, 1824.

Approval and funding in place, William Barney traveled to Annapolis with instructions to secure land at Thomas Point, on which a thirty-foot-tall tower would be built. At this location, the tower would be built more than a mile from deep water, greatly reducing its effectiveness.

At Annapolis, William Barney scouted land at Thomas Point that was owned by Jeremiah Chase, who was related to Barney's wife. On Barney's recommendation, the federal government bought a seven-acre parcel at the tip of the Thomas Point peninsula from Chase for $529.69.

As 1824 turned into 1825, the volume of shipping traffic into and out of Baltimore continued to expand, and the need for a lighthouse at Thomas Point—even the wrong lighthouse—only increased. With the land purchased and a budget in place, William Bedford Barney, who was still firmly in his role as naval officer at Baltimore, turned his attention to finding a lighthouse builder.

TOWERS ON THE SHORE

Darkness reigns at the foot of the lighthouse.
—Japanese proverb

As the Port of Baltimore rose in size and prominence, the city's booming economy depended on a smooth flow of goods into and out of its wharfs and docks. A network of navigational aids, anchored by lighthouses marking major shoals, was sorely needed. Stephen Pleasonton, the man the federal government trusted to oversee the expansion of the lighthouse network, both on the Chesapeake and around the young nation, preferred to delegate much of the responsibility to federal and local officials in the ports and along the coasts. In Baltimore, that official was Captain William Bedford Barney.

Barney oversaw the construction of Maryland's first lighthouse: the Bodkin Island Light. It was a simple stone tower built on a now-eroded island near the mouth of the Patapsco River. Construction on this structure began in 1822, and the process was plagued with structural difficulties. To complete the final phases of the Bodkin Island project and shore up the bulkhead below the tower, Captain Barney turned to John Donahoo, a leading citizen and builder at Havre de Grace, at the northern end of the Chesapeake. Although Bodkin Island was Donahoo's first lighthouse project, he would soon become the leading builder of lighthouses on the Chesapeake Bay.

The Bay's next lighthouse was slated to be built on the Thomas Point shoreline, just five miles from the state capital at Annapolis. While many

The thirty-six-foot-tall Concord Point Lighthouse tower at Havre de Grace, Maryland, was built in 1827 by John Donahoo. Two years earlier, Donohoo had completed the first lighthouse tower at Thomas Point, a thirty-foot-tall stone tower that likely closely resembled the Concord Point tower. *From* Harpers New Monthly Magazine, *vol. 28 (December 1863–May 1864).*

lighthouses were required at remote, dangerous locations, the Thomas Point tower would be set on a peninsula and could be built, manned and serviced with relative ease. A simple design was specified for the spot: a thirty-foot-tall tower built of stone alongside a modest keeper's dwelling and a well. The tower would be eighteen feet across at its base, with stones at the base three feet in thickness. From there, it would taper to nine feet in diameter at the top with twenty-inch-thick stones.

Barney requested bids, and the lowest came in from Donahoo and his partner, Simon Frieze, also of Havre de Grace, Maryland. The pair had never before built a lighthouse from scratch but had been involved in construction projects along the waterfront of the northern Chesapeake, including the Bodkin Island project. On February 25, 1825, Barney and Donahoo signed the contract to stand up a tower at Thomas Point. It would be completed and lit within nine months.

The Bodkin and the Thomas Point towers were, like many of Donahoo's tower lighthouses, straightforward affairs, unadorned and practical, built for the purpose of hosting a light and not as architectural or historic statements. It is likely that the granite for the tower was quarried, cut and shaped on the banks of the Susquehanna River, not far from Donahoo's Havre de Grace base. From there, it was shipped some sixty miles down the Bay to Thomas Point.

While the Chesapeake Bay's northern shoreline is studded with rocks, in the middle Bay, at the Thomas Point peninsula, it is difficult to find any solid material in the ground larger than an oyster shell. The submerged land at the point is sand and mud and naturally prone to erosion and shifts. The shoreline portion of the seven acres Chase sold to the government at Thomas Point was, essentially, a sandbar.

The location on which Donahoo and his crew placed their Thomas Point tower was later described by Stephen Pleasonton as "a clay bank at least 30 feet high and about 500 feet from the water." As described, this location sounded perfectly reasonable, although it is unlikely the tower was actually built at such a high and secure location, especially given what happened in the ensuing fifteen years.

By the end of 1825, the stone tower had been completed. The final price tag was $5,676. Captain Barney, acting as a one-man enterprise with responsibilities ranging from real estate to construction, and now staffing, advertised for and hired the light's first keeper. The tower was first lit, without ceremony, in December 1825.

At the same time he was building the Thomas Point tower, John Donahoo was also building another lighthouse tower for Barney, this one a forty-footer that was set at Pooles Island just north of the Patapsco River. Donahoo would go on to build more than a dozen lighthouse on the Chesapeake Bay; seven of his lighthouses still stand, including the Pooles Island tower.

EVEN AS JOHN DONAHOO and his crew worked on the first Thomas Point tower, Stephen Pleasonton's Lighthouse Establishment was busy building other towers, including a pair at remote locations in south Florida. In 1825, a sixty-five-foot-tall brick tower was constructed nearly 1,000 miles to the south of Thomas Point at Cape Florida. At the same time, 125 miles to the southwest of Cape Florida, a new sixty-five-foot lighthouse tower was constructed at Key West. These southern towers faced unique and real challenges. The Key West tower was eventually destroyed in a major hurricane. In 1836, the Cape Florida tower was attacked by a band of Seminoles who shot holes in a lamp oil storage tank, leading to a major fire that burned away much of the tower's interior and trapped its wounded keeper at the top. Twelve miles away, the crew of a navy schooner heard explosions from the tower and turned to investigate. Upon the discovery of the trapped keeper, the sailors shot a line to the top of the tower and sent up a crew to safely extract the man. The Cape Florida tower stayed dark for the next decade.

Other lighthouse projects undertaken at the same time faced challenges that originated inside Stephen Pleasonton's organization. A forty-foot tower on a bluff at the entrance to Pensacola Bay, Florida, was lit in late 1824,

A section of an 1878 map focused on land, not water, illustrates Thomas Point's relationship to the city of Annapolis, the increasing number of residences reaching out toward the lighthouse site and a break on the south side of Thomas Point. Interestingly, the map shows the light on shore, although the shoal lighthouse had been commissioned three years earlier and the shore tower abandoned at the same time. *U.S. National Archives and Records Administration.*

and mariners were soon complaining about trees obscuring the light. On Lake Huron, a creaky thirty-two-foot-tall tower was lit in April 1825, behind schedule and shockingly over budget. It fell down less than four years later.

Not long after the tower's commissioning, the shortcomings of the new Thomas Point lighthouse, as both a structure and as a navigational aid, became apparent. Built on land procured by an American war hero from a member of the Continental Congress, on the edge of the relatively mild Chesapeake—just five miles from a state capitol building, a mere thirty miles from Stephen Pleasonton's desk at Washington and more than one hundred miles from the open ocean—it had some major problems.

The site that Barney selected, Pleasonton approved, the federal government purchased and Donahoo built on proved dangerously unsuitable. The shoreline beneath and around the tower rapidly eroded. The Bay approached the lighthouse at an alarming rate and pushed irreversibly closer with each storm and full moon high tide. In an attempt to stabilize the situation, piles of rubble were set at the foot of the tower.

By 1838, the Chesapeake had swelled to within fifteen feet of the tower, and the structure was in real danger of being compromised. The tower itself was also a problem. Despite his later success as a lighthouse builder, Donahoo's early inexperience showed in the Thomas Point construction. The tower proved prone to damage from wind and rain. To complicate matters, the tower's light, already located at a distance from shipping and deep water, was sometimes obscured by trees. It proved insufficient as an aid to navigation.

After reviewing the scene at Thomas Point—which should have been a straightforward project when measured against others undertaken by his organization—Stephen Pleasonton, the man ultimately responsible for the situation, told Congress in 1838, "This case shows, as clearly as anything can do, the danger which attends all such establishments."

WILLIAM BEDFORD BARNEY'S CONNECTION with the first lighthouses at Thomas Point is indelible, but in the years after the commissioning of the first Thomas Point lighthouse, his professional career took an unexpected turn, proving that even a well-connected American war hero can suffer at the winds and whims of politics and politicians. Less than four years after the Thomas Point tower was lit, William Bedford Barney was out of a job.

In 1828, Andrew Jackson emerged victorious in a hotly contested presidential election that was largely divided along state lines. In the election, Jackson carried the South, and his political rival, sitting president John Quincy Adams, carried much of the North, including the state of Maryland, where William Barney had publicly supported Adams.

Once in office, President Jackson's "spoils system" became notorious, and William Barney became a target. In April 1829, one month after his inauguration, President Andrew Jackson removed William Barney from his position at Baltimore, presumably due to Barney's support of Adams. Barney's replacement at Baltimore was Dabney S. Carr, a twenty-seven-year-old Virginian and a grandnephew of Thomas Jefferson's.

No official reason was provided for Jackson's move at Baltimore, but the removal of a long-serving son of an American naval hero (and son-in-law of a signer of the Declaration of Independence) generated controversy and anger, especially from within the Barney residence. Mary Chase Barney, at this point the mother of eleven children, suddenly found her husband unemployed, and she responded with outrage. Mrs. Barney lobbied the U.S. Senate, asking it to require Jackson to provide a reason for the firing of her husband. She wrote a sharp protest letter to Jackson that was widely circulated throughout the United States. The letter was so vitriolic that it virtually guaranteed that William Barney would never serve any role in the Jackson administration, but it attracted widespread attention and is now considered to be an important example of early female political activism in American. In her letter, Mrs. Barney confronted the president "for the injury you have inflicted on a meritorious officer and his helpless family." She went on to write that Jackson's administration was "a cancerous excrescence fastened upon the body politic." Emboldened by the positive public response to the letter, Mary Barney continued to publicly criticize Jackson and his administration, even opening a weekly newspaper while pregnant with her twelfth child.

In 1832, the Democratic Party held its first national convention a short distance from the Barney residence at Baltimore. At the convention, Andrew Jackson was nominated for a second term, and he went on to easily win the general election. After nearly three years pursuing the cause, Mary Barney relented and turned her considerable energy and talent toward writing a biography of her father-in-law, Commander Joshua Barney.

William Bedford Barney died in 1838, as the land at the base of the Thomas Point tower rapidly eroded away. He is buried at Baltimore. Mary Chase Barney died in 1872 and is buried at Washington, D.C.

REBUILDING THE SHORE TOWER

The rapid erosion and poor condition of the tower spurred Stephen Pleasonton into action. A well-connected New Englander named Winslow Lewis had been responsible for building the collapsed Michigan tower and the ineffective Pensacola Bay tower, but despite the setbacks, his low prices and speed kept him in the good graces of Stephen Pleasonton, who continued to funnel projects to Lewis. In 1838, Pleasonton's Lighthouse Establishment gave the contract for rebuilding the endangered Thomas Point tower to Winslow Lewis, directing him to take down the old tower and build a new one "in a secure place." This second tower was built using material from the old one and stood on higher ground behind the keeper's cottage, which stayed in place. Lewis added three feet to the top

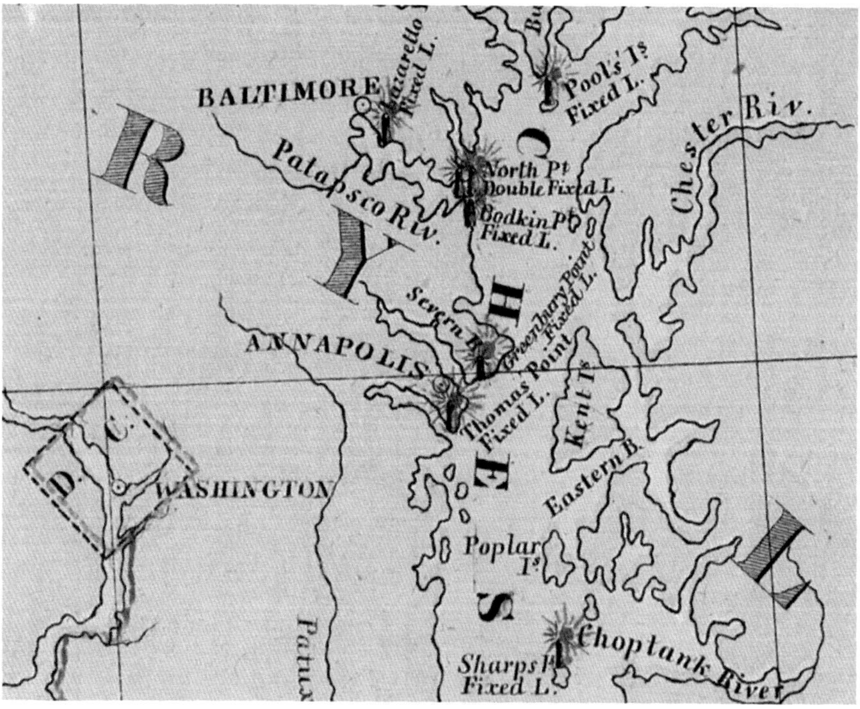

In 1848, Stephen Pleasonton, under fire from mariners and Congress, produced a chart illustrating the lighthouse network that had been established on his watch. This detailed section shows the central Chesapeake Bay and the approaches to Baltimore. The second lighthouse tower on Thomas Point is depicted, although the relative power of the light is likely overstated, as attested by mariners, who frequently complained about its lack of visibility. *Library of Congress.*

of the tower to improve the visibility of the light and was paid $2,000 for the project. This second attempt at a Thomas Point tower was completed and lit in 1840.

THERE ARE FEW RECORDS and accounts of life at the Thomas Point towers. We can surmise that most of the keepers were Annapolis-area residents and that they tended the light in between visits into town for provisions and

Detail of an 1855 U.S. Geological Survey map of the South River area, with unusual orientation. Note Thomas Point beginning to break away from the shoreline. A small bluff at the tip of the point is depicted. *U.S. National Archives and Records Administration.*

entertainment. It must have been a fairly plum assignment, just a few miles from the activity at Annapolis and so far from deep water that minimal, if any, lifesaving or law enforcement activity was required. A commercial oyster trade was developing, and the shoal at Thomas Point, as well as nearby beds, were lined with oysters. It is likely that the Thomas Point keepers enjoyed close relationships with oystermen and that some keepers even plied the trade themselves. The steady paycheck, simple duties, minimal oversight and attractive location make it likely that a close-knit group of locals kept the tower, even after a newly formed Lighthouse Board formalized the national lighthouse network in the 1850s. The list of men who served at the Thomas Point towers is incomplete, but the known keepers include familiar Anne Arundel County surnames such as Wayson, Phelps, Basil and Sappington. The last keeper of the tower received the position in 1874 at age twenty-five. The prior keeper had been his father-in-law.

One interesting anecdote was reported in newspapers in late spring 1841. A Captain Roake was keeping the lighthouse and reported that heavy winds and an attraction to the light drove a "very numerous flock of birds, embracing many varieties," against the walls of the tower. In a chaotic few moments, hundreds of birds were stunned and killed. Among the flock were "woodcocks, redbirds, yellow birds, Indian hens, swallows, owls and other kinds unknown." After recovering from the initial shock, the captain and his assistant surveyed the fallen birds and chose the most promising to broil and make into pies.

JOHN DONAHOO

Overcoming the issues with the first lighthouse he built from start to finish on Thomas Point, John Donahoo quickly established a track record of reliable work at fair prices. Donahoo became a favorite of the Lighthouse Establishment and went on to build ten more lighthouses on the Chesapeake, including the Concord Point Lighthouse in his native Havre de Grace, the oldest lighthouse in Maryland open to public visitors.

Following his death in 1858, John Donahoo was buried at Havre de Grace, less than two miles away from his landmark Concord Point Lighthouse.

Seven of John Donahoo's Chesapeake Bay lighthouses still stand, including:

The Concord Point Light at Havre de Grace, Maryland, was built by John Donahoo in 1827. *Photo by Carol M. Highsmith, Library of Congress.*

- Pooles Island Lighthouse (1825), in the National Register of Historic Places
- Concord Point Lighthouse (1827), in the National Register of Historic Places
- Cove Point Lighthouse (1828), in the National Register of Historic Places
- Point Lookout Lighthouse (1830)
- Turkey Point Lighthouse (1833), in the National Register of Historic Places
- Piney Point Lighthouse (1836), in the National Register of Historic Places
- Fishing Battery Lighthouse (1853), abandoned but standing; fundraising for preservation efforts are underway
- Thomas Point Lighthouse (1825), replaced by second stone tower in 1838
- Fog Point Lighthouse (1827), abandoned in 1875 and later destroyed
- Lazaretto Point Lighthouse (1831), demolished in 1926; a replica was built nearby in 1985

- Clay Island Lighthouse (1832), deactivated in 1892 and collapsed in 1894
- Watts Island Lighthouse (1833), destroyed in a storm in 1944
- Blakistone Island Lighthouse (1851), destroyed by fire in 1956

LENSES, LAMPS AND LANTERNS

A typical arrangement for a lighthouse lighting system involves a lamp, a lens and a lantern. The lamp is the actual source of the light. The lens fits over the lamp and, when properly designed and tended, expands and illuminates the light generated by the lamp. The lantern is the container or fitting that surrounds and protects the lamp and lens. At the Thomas Point Shoal Lighthouse, and at many other lighthouses, the lantern is the glass-paneled room at the top of the structure.

Winslow Lewis, the sea captain and inventor who rebuilt the first Thomas Point tower, had recognized the growth of the American lighthouse system years earlier and moved to make himself indispensable to all phases of the network's infrastructure. In 1812, before Stephen Pleasonton took his position at the head of the Lighthouse Establishment, Lewis developed a lighting system that he patented and then sold to the U.S. government. The system was relatively crude, but it was fuel efficient and could be mass produced, keeping costs down. The enterprising Lewis spent the next four years fitting his lamps in American lighthouses. In 1825, Lewis installed his proprietary lighting system into the new Thomas Point tower. A Lewis system would attempt to mark the shoal for the next three decades.

The Lewis system comprised thirteen separate lamps and a series of sixteen-inch reflectors. Tending the fragile system challenged the poorly trained lighthouse keepers. A Congressionally sponsored investigation later found that, among other faults, the abrasive powder supplied to keepers for cleaning the system's reflectors rubbed off their silver coating, leading to a difficult choice for the keepers: dirty reflectors or no reflective coating. Neither scenario enhanced the quality of the light.

A fuel source is required to power a lighthouse lamp. Historically, everything from sperm whale oil to lard to kerosene has been used for this purpose. For more than a century, the challenges and expenses associated with procuring, transporting and storing lamp fuel were a major concern for those charged with developing and maintaining the American lighthouse network. Managing the fluctuating price and availability of lamp fuel, especially the clean and bright-burning sperm whale oil that was in favor through the first half of the nineteenth century, was a constant challenge for the Lighthouse Establishment. Yet even as he installed his lighting systems around the nation, Winslow Lewis gained a near monopoly on sperm whale oil, further strengthening his connection to and profits from the growing lighthouse network.

Looking to further expand his business, Winslow Lewis began building lighthouses, and once Stephen Pleasonton came into power, the pair formed a sort of alliance. Lewis was soon the busiest lighthouse builder in America, and Pleasonton, ever mindful of his budgets, seemed pleased with Lewis's ability to complete towers quickly and cheaply—the disastrous Michigan project notwithstanding. Lewis developed standardized lighthouse sizing and plans, with most structures built of brick and, occasionally, stone. However, cheap and fast can come at a price, and the lighthouses built by Lewis and his crews often proved to be poorly constructed. Only a few survive. The Thomas Point tower rebuild, which Lewis completed in 1830, eventually fell down.

By the 1830s, a new lighting technology had emerged from Europe and proved vastly superior to Lewis's lamps. Despite clear evidence and public pressure, Stephen Pleasonton resisted the innovation. The working relationship between Winslow Lewis and Stephen Pleasonton, always a source of suspicion among mariners and shipping interests, came under increased scrutiny.

In 1820s France, as Winslow Lewis's flawed system was being fitted at American lighthouses, a physicist named Augustin Fresnel was working at the behest of the French Commission for Lighthouses and developed a breakthrough new lens. In an extended series of experiments, Fresnel methodically arranged a series of cut-glass prisms around a brass frame.

The Fourth Order Fresnel lens installed at Thomas Point Shoal Lighthouse in 1899 was removed when the station was automated in 1986 and it is now in safekeeping in the Coast Guard offices at Curtis Bay, near Baltimore. *U.S. Coast Guard.*

The resulting shape resembled a pineapple, and when a lamp was placed inside, the superior quality of the light it produced was undeniable.

Fresnel's new lenses were heavy, large and difficult to transport, but their effectiveness was extraordinary. The heavy glass prisms, while subject to damage by direct blows, promised a lifespan certain to be longer than any fragile lamp and reflector system. The French-built lenses were also expensive, although the initial cost was offset by reduced fuel consumption—Fresnel's lens worked so well that less lamp fuel was needed to produce an appropriate beam. Fresnel's lenses quickly became the new lighthouse standard.

Across the Atlantic, American seamen and shipping industry leaders knew that the U.S. lighthouse and navigation aids lagged far behind those in Europe and immediately began advocating for the new Fresnel lens. But Stephen Pleasonton resisted the European technology and stayed with Lewis lamps, much to the dismay of mariners. The publishers of the widely referenced *American Coast Pilot* were especially vocal in their criticism of Lewis's engineering and Pleasonton's decisions. A pair of naval officers were dispatched by Congress to Europe, charged with studying the more advanced system of navigation aids and the technology behind them. By 1837, the complaints had moved Congress to conduct an investigation and take action. Stephen Pleasonton was cut out of many major decisions around new lighthouse construction.

In 1841, at the specific request of Congress, a Fresnel lens was installed at the Navesink Twin Lights in New Jersey, but the general adoption was slow. In the 1840s, Congress, at the urging of mariners, forced a test of lenses. Even after the Fresnel lens proved superior in the testing, Stephen Pleasonton continued to resist—the new lenses were too expensive and too difficult for lighthouse keepers to maintain. In March 1851, Congress ordered an investigation of the American lighthouse system. When the investigation's report was released, ten months later, it called the Fresnel "greatly superior to any other mode of light-house illumination." The report would lead to a long-overdue house-cleaning process at the Lighthouse Establishment.

A NEW LIGHTHOUSE AUTHORITY

As the political storm around lighthouses and lenses brewed in nearby Washington, the shipping trade into and out of Baltimore thrived, both to Europe and, in even greater volume, to South America. In the prosperous decade before the American Civil War, Caribbean and South American coffee, sugar, molasses and copper flowed up the Chesapeake Bay, while lumber, coal, granite, hogs and, most importantly, flour were exported from Baltimore. By 1851, one-third of all coffee imported into the United States came through Baltimore, and seven different companies maintained coffee fleets at Baltimore.

In addition to regional lines across both shores of the Chesapeake Bay, regular steam and sail lines operated between Baltimore and Boston, Providence, Hartford, New York, Norfolk, Richmond, Charleston, Savannah, New Orleans and other, smaller, ports. The West Coast of North America also became part of the Baltimore trade. In 1850, forty-four ships cleared from Baltimore bound for San Francisco.

Immigrants from Europe poured into Baltimore, mostly German and Irish. Many of these immigrants quickly found work building canals and railroads. A reputable steamer coming to America from Germany could carry up to two hundred passengers in steerage, and the trip typically took about one month. A full return cargo to Europe, often tobacco, could reliably be arranged.

As the need for a reliable system of navigation aids expanded—not only on the Chesapeake Bay but now also on the Pacific coast, the Gulf Coast,

The oyster wharf at Pratt Street in Baltimore, circa 1905. *Library of Congress.*

the Great Lakes and along the busy length of the East Coast—the outcry concerning the longstanding leadership of Stephen Pleasonton reached a fever pitch.

The Congressional investigation, conducted from 1851 into 1852, proved blistering and noted that "there has never been an efficient, systematic plan of construction, illumination, inspection, and superintendence of lights, etc. in the United States.... [T]he illuminating apparatus in the United States is of a description now nearly obsolete throughout all maritime countries."

The report called Pleasonton's organization "defective" and noted that "it is plainly impossible to direct from a bureau at Washington the light-house construction and illumination of an extended coast, no part of which is visited by the directing officer, who has besides no knowledge of the principles of optics, of chemistry, or of engineering."

In 1852, Congress completely removed Stephen Pleasonton from the Lighthouse Establishment and formed a new Lighthouse Board to oversee the entire system. The new board would remain under the Treasury Department, but it would comprise accomplished men with backgrounds appropriate for the work at hand. The initial board, seated in 1851, included representatives from the U.S. Navy, the U.S. Topographical Engineers, the U.S. Coast Survey and the Smithsonian Institution. They immediately moved into action. Future lighthouse sites would be chosen by trained engineers. Procedures and training were formalized and documented. Replacing Winslow Lewis's proprietary system with new Fresnel lenses was a top priority, as was finding a new source of lamp fuel; the price and availability of sperm whale oil were too unpredictable.

The new Lighthouse Board acted quickly and efficiently. At the request of mariners, five new buoys were placed at dangerous points in the Chesapeake between Thomas Point and the mouth of the Patapsco River in 1854.

The following year, a modern Fifth-Order Fresnel lens was installed atop the tower at Thomas Point, followed by a more powerful Fourth-Order Fresnel lens in 1857. In 1858, the channel into Baltimore was dredged to a depth that would accommodate new, larger steamships.

A standardized color and buoy system was developed, and updates to those aids were immediately published in a systematic manner. With the price of sperm whale oil dramatically rising, the Lighthouse Board began a conversion to lard oil fuel; this was soon abandoned, as easily sourced, relatively inexpensive kerosene became the standard for lamp fuel.

As the Lighthouse Board acted boldly with regard to modernizing lenses and procedures, an innovative new lighthouse construction method was developed in Europe. The system allowed lighthouses to be built quickly, relatively inexpensively and, most importantly, out over the water, atop a set of pilings that were screwed into the bottom. The new method was closely studied and then attempted in the United States, although the coming Civil War would delay its deployment.

At the dawn of the American Civil War, the loyalties of the State of Maryland and its largest cities were divided. At Annapolis, the United States Naval Academy was shuttered, and midshipmen from Southern states were sent home. The remaining students were sent north to Newport, Rhode

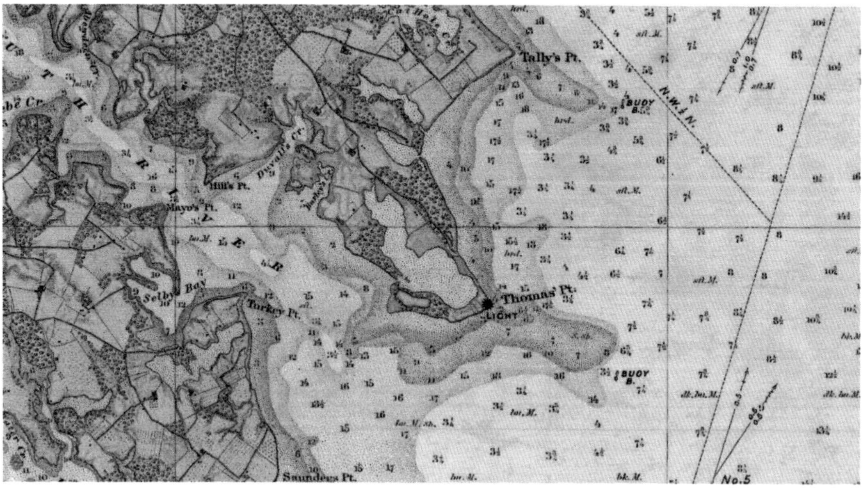

Detail of an 1862 nautical chart showing the lighthouse tower at the tip of Thomas Point and an unlit buoy positioned at the end of the shoal. Note the Thomas Point peninsula, already showing a break west of the lighthouse and increasingly narrow northwest of the lighthouse. *U.S. National Archives and Records Administration.*

Island, away from the war. Federal troops who arrived at Annapolis to secure the academy and the state capital were openly mocked, and their passage in and out of town by rail was frequently delayed by sabotage.

At Baltimore, some locals attacked Union troops as they passed through the city. The Confederates coveted the city, its port and its shipping infrastructure. In the early phase of the conflict, Union forces moved in to extinguish any smoldering Rebel sympathies and secure the city, which they accomplished in the spring of 1861. Although the infrastructure of the port itself remained intact throughout the war, as did the system of navigational aids in Maryland's Chesapeake Bay, many aids, to the South, were destroyed by Confederate troops and sympathizers. The war had brought the shipping business to a crawl. While the port remained open and no Confederate operations were conducted on the northern Chesapeake, many of the connecting railroad lines into the interior were impassable. Without access to the valuable material sourced to the south and west, Baltimore's shipping sharply declined.

IN FEBRUARY 1865, PRESIDENT Abraham Lincoln traveled to Annapolis from Washington by rail and there boarded a steamship for the passage south to Hampton Roads, Virginia, where he would attend a peace conference with Confederate leaders. Speed was of the essence, and Lincoln and his small traveling party were set to travel into Confederate waters aboard the steamer *Thomas Colyer*. This vessel had been seized by the federal government at Alexandria, Virginia, four years earlier and was considered among the Union's fastest. The imposing sidewheel steamer *Herman Livingston*, chartered by the United States Navy, was scheduled to meet the *Colyer* off Annapolis and would push hard to keep up on the passage south. A reporter from the *New York Herald* was with the president aboard the *Colyer*. His front-page story, published on February 5, 1865, includes a familiar midwinter scene at Thomas Point.

Shortly after the *Colyer*'s midafternoon departure from Annapolis, and upon reaching the open Bay, the *Herald* correspondent reported, "[W]e encountered large fields of Ice, through which we passed slowly, and in which we met the steamer *Herman Livingston* off Thomas' Point Shoals at twenty-five minutes past two."

IN THE WAKE OF the Civil War's end, the Port of Baltimore roared back, and new shipping lines were established linking the city with major European ports, including Rotterdam, Antwerp and Liverpool. By the late 1860s, a German passenger could purchase a single ticket ensuring him a transatlantic passage to Baltimore by ship, followed by a railroad journey inland. In 1868, ten thousand immigrants sailed up the Chesapeake to Baltimore. The big new steamers that plied the Atlantic required large amounts of coal, and Baltimore, with its direct connection into coal-rich West Virginia and Pennsylvania, became an important center for refueling and exports. The B&O Railroad's western expansion resumed, and by 1875, it had reached Chicago, 811 miles to the northwest. The flour exports to Brazil resumed, as did the tobacco exports to Europe. The Chesapeake Bay shipping channel was busier than ever, and there were no signs of it slowing. With the increased traffic moving near the shoal, the short tower on Thomas Point continued to be a problem. A report to Congress painted a desperate picture of the scene on the peninsula:

> *The light-house at Thomas's Point…can serve but poorly its purpose as a warning of the dangerous shoal that makes out from its distance of one and a quarter miles into the Bay…its present location is such that little use can be made of it at night, and in times of foggy or thick weather it is utterly useless…The outer extremity of the shoal is marked only by a buoy and it*

> *is a matter of frequent occurrence to see vessels ashore here. The ineligibility of its present location is frequently the source of complaint by mariners.*

The condition of the tower and residence was also discussed:

> *This station is also in a bad state of repair. The rain, in windy weather, beats through the old masonry of the tower, flooding the inside of the structure and frequently damaging the material in charge of the keeper.*

After nearly fifty years on the point, the tower had become glaringly insufficient. The route to and from Baltimore was only getting busier, and the Lighthouse Board was finally ready to take the needed action at Thomas Point.

SCREWPILES ON THE SHOALS

The lighthouse and lightship appeal to the interests and better instinct of man because they are symbolic of never-ceasing watchfulness, of steadfast endurance in every exposure, of widespread helpfulness. The building and the keeping of the lights is a picturesque and humanitarian work of the nation.
—George Rockwell Putnam, commissioner of lighthouses, 1910–35

With the Port of Baltimore making real and positive impact on the local, state and federal economies, the Lighthouse Board made necessarily bold proposals to solve the problems at Thomas Point. The first order of business was relocating the light. In the years since the tower's original construction, new technology had developed that made the concept of a relatively inexpensive lighthouse built *over* water, out on the *end* of the shoal and *near* the shipping lanes a real possibility.

In 1872, the Lighthouse Board brought a new plan for Thomas Point to Congress. After calling the existing shore tower "utterly useless," the board unveiled the new proposal for Thomas Point:

> *A light-house on the point of the shoal, in 8 feet of water, which will be distant from the shore about one and a quarter miles, is recommended for this place. The new light-house should be provided with a fog-bell, the want of which is another defect at the old station, as the distance from the track of vessels going up or down the bay is so great that it would be useless if put there, as it could not be heard.... If a light-house were built at the place referred to, viz, near the outer extremity of the shoal, and provided with a*

> *fog-bell, it would supply a defect long felt by the commerce of Chesapeake Bay, and render the maintenance of an almost useless light unnecessary.*

The fastest and least expensive method of building a lighthouse over water had come to the United States from England, where Alexander Mitchell, a blind Irish engineer, had conceived and built a novel new lighthouse on shifting sands at the mouth of the River Thames. Mitchell's lighthouse, lit in 1841, was a breakthrough, and it sat in a high-profile, heavily trafficked stretch of water. Word quickly spread among mariners and lighthouse authorities. In areas with soft, relatively shallow bottoms, a house and lantern structure could be set atop a series of iron pilings that were literally screwed into the bottom. Once in place, the screws, typically with blades three to four feet in diameter, proved incredibly secure.

Alexander Mitchell's innovation was warmly received by the public. The July 23, 1842 edition of England's popular *Penny Magazine of the Society for the Diffusion of Useful Knowledge* featured an article titled "Recent Improvements in Lighthouses." The article called Mitchell's new screwpile lighthouse concept "[o]ne of the most remarkable applications of the screw ever perhaps attempted" and went on to enthuse:

> *Here is a structure entirely supported by seven posts or piles driven, not into firm rock, but into loose sand, or at least loam, which has hitherto baffled the efforts of engineers to render it stable and firm.... The main structure, too, instead of presenting to the violence of the waves a surface which has in some instances, been supposed to be exposed to a pressure of one hundred tons, consists only of the skeleton frame-work, presenting the least amount of resisting surface. One of the most remarkable circumstances connected with this mode of construction is the celerity with which the various parts can be put up.*

Out on the water, screwpiles could take the place of expensively maintained, manned lightships and of buoys and beacons with insufficient or no lights. Lighthouses built to Alexander Mitchell's concept began to appear in shallow waters in western Europe and soon drew the attention of the American Lighthouse Establishment, which was, in the wake of Stephen Pleasonton's tenure, proving keen to adopt the superior European lighthouse technology. Mitchell consulted on the United States' first screwpile, lit in 1850 near the mouth of the Delaware Bay. Soon screwpiles were under construction in shallow, soft-bottomed areas around the eastern United States.

Immediately following the Civil War, the Lighthouse Board built out a lighthouse depot at Lazaretto Point in Baltimore. Sections of new lighthouses were fabricated at this site and loaded onto vessels for transport to final locations. *U.S. National Archives and Records Administration.*

Officials with the Fifth District of the United States Lighthouse Board, based at Baltimore, were especially interested in screwpiles. The design seemed perfect for the shallow waters of the Chesapeake Bay and the sounds of North Carolina, all of which were within their purview. Iron screwpile infrastructure could be forged at Baltimore or brought to the lighthouse depot the board had established at Baltimore's Lazeretto Point via rail or ship. Large sections of the screwpile cottages could be prefabricated at Lazaretto and then shipped to their final locations to be reassembled over the water. The Chesapeake's first screwpile was lit in 1855 at Seven Foot Knoll, near the entrance to the Patapsco River and Baltimore. While the Civil War slowed down the deployment of screwpiles on the Chesapeake, the years following the war featured a flurry of building activity.

In 1872, with a screwpile in mind for Thomas Point Shoal, the Lighthouse Board made its request of Congress: "It is recommended, therefore, that an appropriation be made to build a light-house on Thomas's Point Shoal, supplied with a fog-bell, to take the place of a light-house on Thomas's Point. The estimated cost is $20,000." The appropriation was granted on March 3, 1873. The 2020 value of $20,000 is about $427,000.

The Lighthouse Board would soon learn the flaws of the screwpile design.

THE RIGHT SPOT, THE WRONG LIGHTHOUSE

An especially cold winter of 1872–73 gripped the Chesapeake Bay during the months between the funding of the new Thomas Point Shoal Lighthouse and the start of construction. An incident late that winter at a new screwpile at Love Point, about twelve miles northeast of Thomas Point, brought the flaws of the popular design into sharp focus. The Love Point screwpile, in the words of a Lighthouse Board report, "sustained considerable injury from fields of heavy, floating ice." Ice floes damaged two of the main screwpile supports, leaving the house vulnerable to being carried away or destroyed. After inspecting the damage, officials with the Lighthouse Board grew concerned because they were planning to build a lighthouse of this same style at the more exposed Thomas Point Shoal location. Experts began considering that perhaps a caisson-style lighthouse, more solid but more expensive, would be appropriate for Thomas Point.

A caisson lighthouse is a heavy cylinder, typically built of cast iron on land and then transported horizontally to the final location. There it is placed upright on the bottom and allowed to sink down onto a foundation, sometimes natural and sometimes man-made with pilings. The Chesapeake Bay's first caisson-style lighthouse had been lit in 1873 just south of the Patapsco River. That site, at the main channel into Baltimore, had been originally slated to receive a screwpile, but the location was deemed too important to risk losing the light to ice floes. Placing screwpiles at important locations in the center of the Chesapeake Bay was a risky proposition.

Concerned about the original approved Thomas Point plan, the Lighthouse Board reapproached Congress with a different idea for location. The change in plans is recorded in the Lighthouse Board's October 14, 1873 report to Congress. "The location on the extreme point of the shoal is one of great exposure," the board wrote. The revised proposal continued, "With the experience of Love Point light-house during the winter of 1872–73 before us, it was deemed expedient to change the plan of this light-house, that instead of building it on screwpile, as was first intended, to build a more solid structure, that could be depended upon at all times to safely withstand the heavy ice-floes that form above it in the Bay."

"A cast iron tube filled with concrete" was now desired. Plans had already been drawn up, and engineers had studied the floor of the Bay on the end of the shoal to determine where and how the tube could best be sunk. However, the report admitted, "This light-house will cost considerably more than one on screwpiles and an additional appropriation of $25,000 is therefore required."

The request was denied, and in the absence of this additional funding, the Thomas Point project was suspended. The Lighthouse Board reassessed its plan at Thomas Point, and the project's suspension proved short-lived. The need for a lighthouse on the shoal was far too great.

On March 3, 1875, Congress approved $15,000 in additional funding for the new shoal lighthouse at Thomas Point. It was only enough to build a screwpile, albeit a stronger version than what had previously been built on the Chesapeake.

Before any construction could begin, the federal government needed to officially obtain rights to the land on which it intended to build. The State of Maryland technically owned all the Bay bottom at Thomas Point, but it was willing to sign a bit over to the federal government for the purpose of a lighthouse. In April 1874, Maryland's General Assembly passed an act to "provide for the relinquishment to the United States in certain cases of title to and jurisdiction over lands for sites of lighthouses, beacons, buoys, and floating guides on the coast and in the Waters of this State." On October 28, 1874, five acres of submerged land near the end of the Thomas Point Shoal were conveyed from the State of Maryland to the federal government. A specific spot was referenced by latitude and longitude.

ALTHOUGH THE LIGHTHOUSE AT the end of the Thomas Point Shoal was long overdue and its location, a prominent point near Annapolis, was of a high profile, it was another lighthouse project, nearly two hundred miles to the south, that captured attention along the Baltimore waterfront in a way that no bread-and-butter Chesapeake Bay projects could.

Just south of the mouth of the Chesapeake, about two hundred ship miles from Baltimore's inner harbor, lie the Outer Banks of Virginia and North Carolina. It is a remote coastline vexed by shoals and regularly proving capable of disrupting shipping, especially in the decades before aids to navigation were posted along the length of the coast. Southbound ships, hugging the coastline to avoid the endless northbound rush of the Gulf Stream, were particularly vulnerable. The responsibility for shepherding mariners safely along this coastline fell to the Fifth District of the Lighthouse Board. Despite the demand for other projects, nowhere was the need for a new station more pressing than at Currituck, North Carolina, just south of the Virginia border.

The leaders of the Fifth District aimed to close the gaps of dark coastline along the Outer Banks with a series of lighthouses strung along the coast at a frequency that ensured a mariner would never be without a reference light. In late 1874, the Fifth District submitted a request for funding for a new Currituck tower to Congress. The request was accompanied by a list of forty-eight vessels that had gone ashore at Currituck. The funding was granted.

The new Currituck Beach Lighthouse was well to the south of Baltimore Harbor; however, throughout 1875, updates on the building of this distant tower filled broad swaths of newspapers and dominated conversation along the city's waterfront. In April, the *Baltimore Sun* reminded its readers, "Currituck beach is one of the most dangerous points on the Virginia coast, as was evidenced by the number of marine disasters last fall and winter." Another article reminded Baltimoreans that in the previous twenty-two years, some fifty-six vessels had gone ashore at Currituck—everything from steamships to schooners, "many of them being totally lost." Nearly half of those vessels had been inbound for Baltimore, a pace of losses averaging more than one per year. The *Sun* surmised, "The loss to insurance companies and owners probably would aggregate a million dollars…cast away upon that treacherous coast."

The toothy stretch at Currituck lay along the southern approaches to the mouth of the Chesapeake Bay, and through those approaches came and went the ships composing Baltimore's important Caribbean, South American and Pacific trade. Through much of the nineteenth century, Baltimore's trade with South America dwarfed its trade with Europe. Baltimore was well connected with points south in part because the port was a day or two closer to the southern destinations than rival New York, but more importantly, railroads and well-developed roads connected Baltimore with the fertile inland of Maryland, Virginia, West Virginia and Pennsylvania. Grain from the region, especially when ground into fine flour, was in great demand, especially in booming Brazil. Ships left Baltimore bound for southern ports heavy with grain and flour, and they returned loaded with coffee, sugar, molasses, copper and guano. Barring encounters with shoals and storms, the round trip was efficient and quite lucrative.

The *Baltimore Sun* was eager to supply updates on the new Outer Banks tower. In April, the newspaper noted that the tower "will complete the chain of lights in the new system." In June, the *Sun* reported that construction on the Currituck tower had reached a second window, sixty-five feet off the ground. The paper added that the Currituck light "is to be 160 feet high, an altitude greater than that of any light-house in the fifth district, except the one on Cape Hatteras."

From the rowdy sailor pubs of Baltimore's Fells Point to the mansions of the city's leafy northern suburbs, news of the Currituck tower was well received. Meanwhile, plans for the more modest Thomas Point Shoal screwpile quietly moved forward.

BUILDING THE LIGHTHOUSE ON THE SHOAL

I can think of no other edifice constructed by man as altruistic as a lighthouse. They were built only to serve.
—*George Bernard Shaw*

In April 1875, as the ambitious tower project on the North Carolina coast soaked up money, attention and newspaper ink, workers at the Malster & Donnell iron foundry, in the heart of Baltimore's Fells Point, were completing ironwork for a pair of new Chesapeake screwpile lighthouses: one destined for Tangier Sound and the other for Virginia's York River. Nearby, at the Lighthouse Board's Lazaretto Depot, sections of the cottages that would sit atop the iron bases were prebuilt. Once the entire kits were inspected and approved, they were loaded aboard the Lighthouse Board's steam-powered tender *Tulip* and moved to their final destinations, where they were assembled. It was an efficient new method of construction, and as Baltimore's port expanded, any method of improving the lighting system along the Chesapeake and its approaches was welcomed by shipping interests.

In early 1875, with site and funding secured, the U.S. Lighthouse Board published specifications for the new screwpile lighthouse at Thomas Point, including detailed drawings of the parts required to build it. Concurrently published were specifications for a new screwpile planned for Port Tobacco Flats on the Potomac River, about fifty river miles below Alexandria, Virginia. Fifteen proposals were received for the metalwork for the new screwpiles,

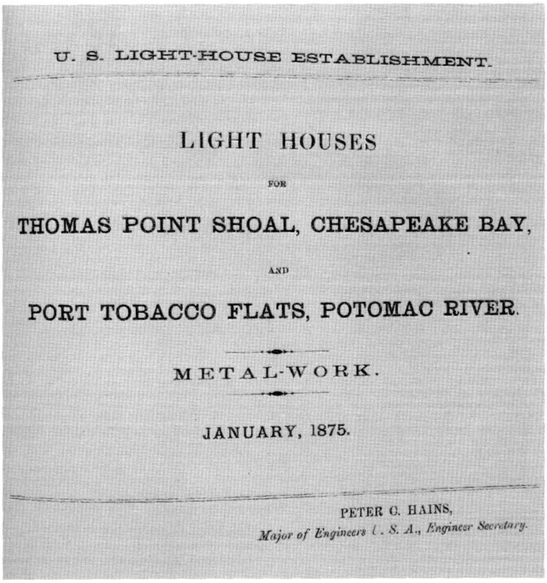

U. S. LIGHT-HOUSE ESTABLISHMENT.

LIGHT HOUSES

FOR

THOMAS POINT SHOAL, CHESAPEAKE BAY,

AND

PORT TOBACCO FLATS, POTOMAC RIVER.

METAL-WORK.

JANUARY, 1875.

PETER C. HAINS,
Major of Engineers U. S. A., Engineer Secretary.

In January 1875, the Lighthouse Board published specifications for metalwork for two new screwpiles it planned to build in 1875: Thomas Point Shoal near Annapolis and one at Port Tobacco Flats on the Potomac. *U.S. National Archives and Records Administration.*

with a high bid of $30,300 and a low bid, from the Atlantic Steam Engine Works of Brooklyn, New York, at $17,400. In late May, the Lighthouse Board announced that the Atlantic Steam Engine Works had been awarded the contracts for the ironwork at Thomas Point and Port Tobacco.

The General Description of the new Thomas Point Shoal Lighthouse begins, "The structure will consist of two parts—the lower, an open framework of iron, forming the foundation, and the upper a frame building, affording quarters for the keepers; the latter is to be surmounted by a lantern, in which is to be placed the illuminating apparatus." The initial specifications are deeply detailed and include instructions all the way down to the door handles.

The specifications call for eight ten-inch piles "of the best quality of wrought-iron" to be screwed vertically into the shoal at a depth of ten feet, including one at the center of the foundation. The screws themselves were specified to be cast iron with a three-foot exterior diameter and two blades, each with a pitch of twelve inches.

Atop the foundation would be a hexagonal house constructed of wood and reachable by two sets of iron stairs, as well as by ladders from the boarding platform. The light would be placed forty-three feet above the average water height. The house would be topped by a copper roof.

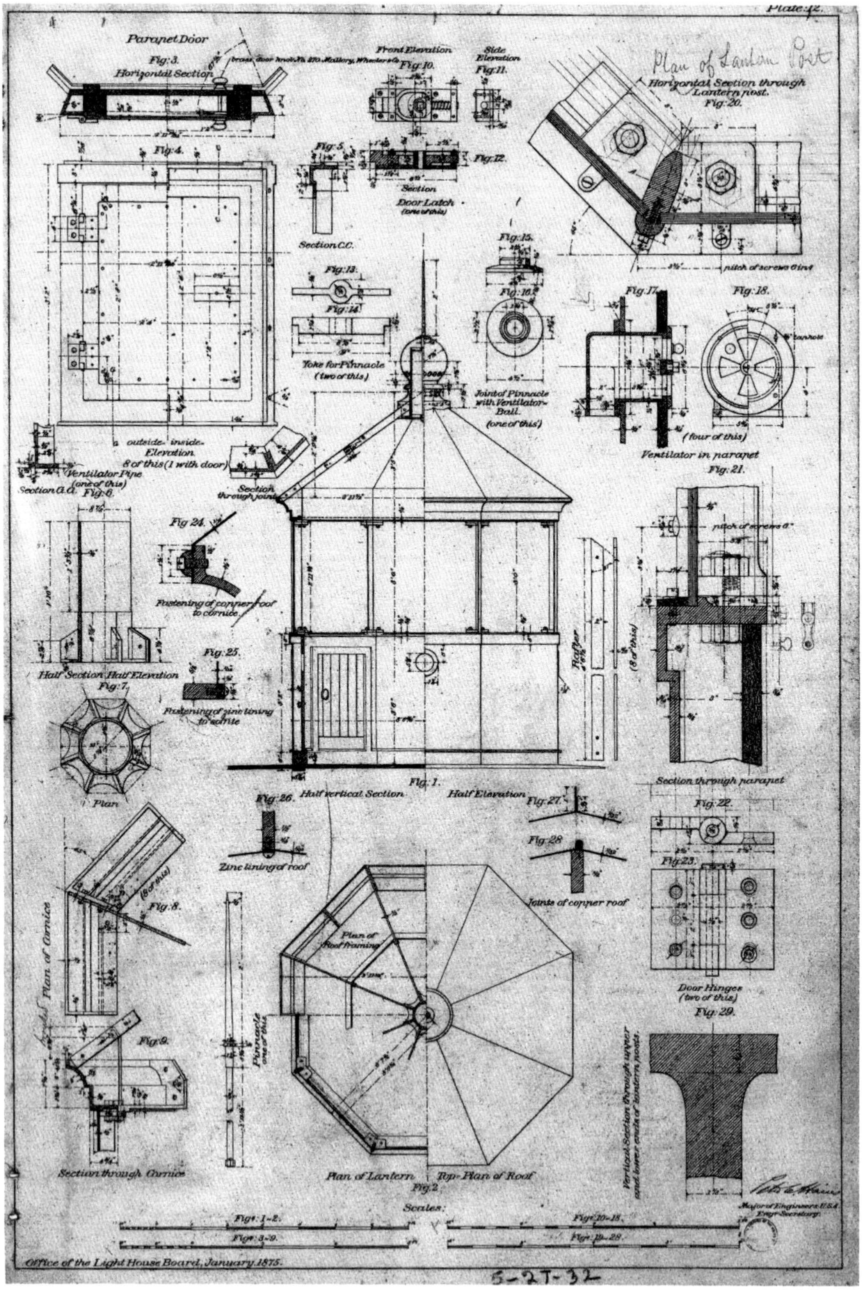

Lantern room plans for the Thomas Point Shoal screwpile lighthouse, as illustrated in plans published by the U.S. Lighthouse Board in January 1875. *U.S. National Archives and Records Administration.*

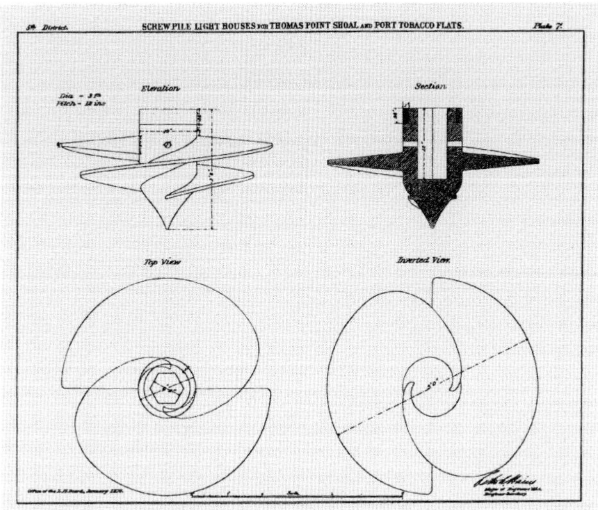

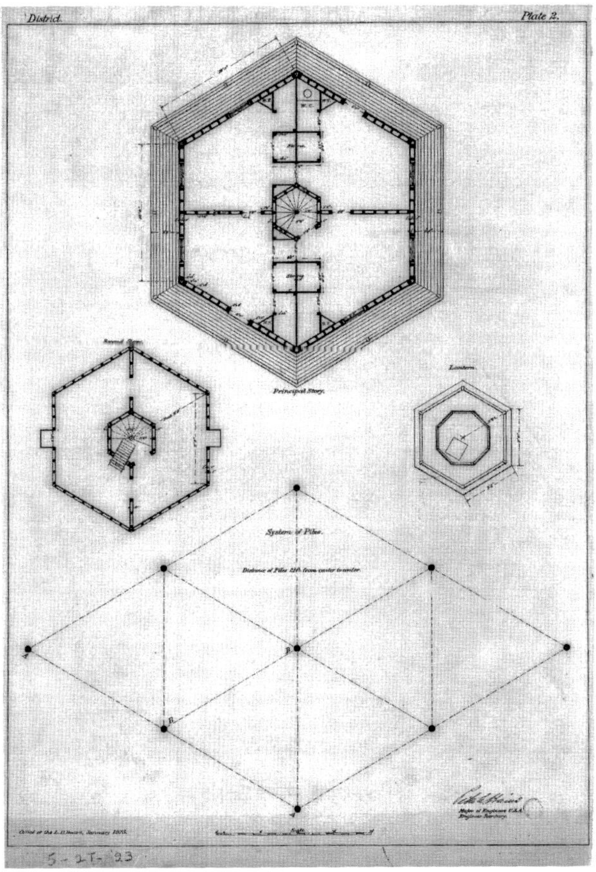

Top: Details of the screws for the Thomas Point Shoal screwpile lighthouse, as illustrated in plans published by the U.S. Lighthouse Board in January 1875. *U.S. National Archives and Records Administration.*

Bottom: Overview of the plans for the hexagonal screwpile lighthouse at Thomas Point Shoal, as published by the U.S. Lighthouse Board in January 1875. *U.S. National Archives and Records Administration.*

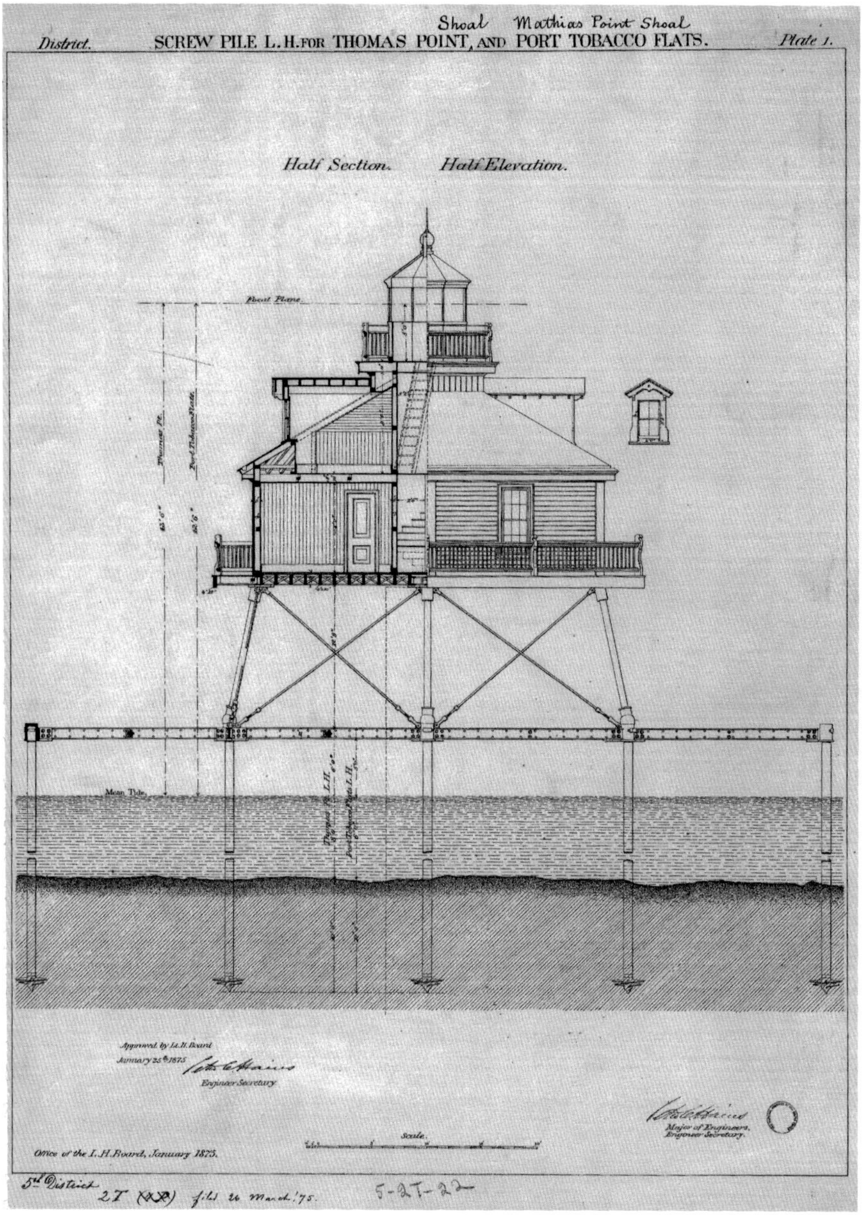

Half section showing the complete structure, above and below water, to be built at Thomas Point Shoal, as illustrated in plans published by the U.S. Lighthouse Board in January 1875. *U.S. National Archives and Records Administration.*

IN 1863, THE LIGHTHOUSE Board established a depot at Baltimore on a five-acre plot that had formerly housed a smallpox hospital and alongside John Donahoo's 1831 Lazaretto Lighthouse tower. The plans to build out the Lazaretto Depot were delayed by the Civil War, but after the war, the depot buzzed with activity. Buoys were assembled and maintained at the site, as were lighthouse sections. The metal for the Thomas Point structure likely came through this depot, where it was assembled and coated with hot linseed oil. Representatives from the Lighthouse Board then inspected and approved the ironwork. After inspection, the iron received two coats of paint and was then greased with a coat of tallow and lead. Small parts such as nuts and bolts were boxed for travel. Only then was the whole package ready for transport out to the shoal.

As specified in a January 1875 document produced by the Lighthouse Establishment for prospective contractors, the Thomas Point Lighthouse kit included 126 metal pieces:

8 Wrought-iron periphery and outstanding piles.
1 Wrought-iron center pile.
9 Cast-iron screws.
16 Double-channel iron struts.
8 Cast-iron struts.
1 Center socket.
2 Sockets with flanges for three struts.
4 Sockets with flanges for four struts.
2 Sockets for outstanding piles.
1 Center column.
6 Periphery columns.
1 Central upper socket.
6 Upper sockets.
24 Tension-rods.
6 Radial beams.
6 Periphery beams.
6 Cast-iron double-shoes and bolts for gallery beams.
12 Gallery tie-rods.
4 Davits with cast iron steps and wrought-iron upper bearings, with struts and bolts.
1 Lantern with cast-iron parapet.
2 Sets of ladders with platforms.

Cast-iron screw on display beneath the relocated Hooper Strait screwpile lighthouse at the Chesapeake Bay Maritime Museum in St. Michaels, Maryland. *Photo by the author.*

Before construction at Thomas Point began, the sister screwpile originally planned for the Port Tobacco Flats was moved across the Potomac to Mathias Point. It was set about three miles away from the first planned location and in a much better position to aid traffic to and from Washington and Alexandria. The Mathias Point Lighthouse was eventually completed in 1876 and closely resembled the Thomas Point Shoal screwpile, although the lighthouse on the Potomac was adorned with additional decorative detail. The Mathias Point screwpile, a true sister to the Thomas Point Shoal screwpile, was automated in 1951 and its cottage dismantled in 1961. A beacon is now mounted atop the original foundational structure, forty-four feet off the surface of the Potomac.

Prior to its construction, the location of the Thomas Point screwpile was also moved, but in a more subtle manner.

FILED SAFELY AT THE National Archives in Washington, D.C., and available for public review, is an undated, uncredited chart labeled "Site of Thomas' Point Shoal LH." The chart was drawn in, or prior to, 1875 for the purpose of illustrating the location of the new lighthouse at the end of the Thomas Point Shoal that would stand offshore compared to its shore-bound predecessor.

The chart features soundings of the water depth, and the markings crowd together as they approach the site of the lighthouse project. A few place names and nearby buoys are called out in detail: Cat Hole Creek, Tally's Point, South River, Greenbury's Point and, of course, Thomas' Point. The then-existing tower lighthouse on the peninsula is also marked. A thin blur of pale blue watercolor marks the shoreline.

The central focus of the chart is drawn roughly in the center of the sheet: the site of the new lighthouse. In the absence of contextual information, it is impossible to know if this rendering was a simple illustration used to show elected officials and members of the public the general location of the new lighthouse, or if it was the official chart provided to the crew who were to build the lighthouse. Noteworthy, however, is the specificity of the new lighthouse location as shown on the chart, including a description of the site prescribed in degrees, minutes and seconds of longitude and latitude.

The latitude and longitude of the site as described in the original deed conveying the Bay bottom from Maryland to the federal government and on the chart reads:

38 54' 03" North Latitude
76 25' 35" West Longitude

A pair of red dashed lines extend toward the center of the chart from these listings. The red lines converge at the tip of the Thomas Point Shoal, where a cartographer penciled in the circular "sun" symbol the Lighthouse Board used to denote its lighthouses. A second of latitude covers about ninety feet. A second of longitude, in the vicinity of Annapolis, is about seventy-nine feet. The chart and the original deed depict a lighthouse that was to be built at a very specific location.

The water depth at the listed location is actually about forty feet deep, not the six or seven feet depicted on the chart. It is well offshore of the end of the shoal, closer to the shipping channel. The actual position of Thomas Point Shoal Lighthouse, as built and standing today, is about one thousand feet farther south and about half a mile farther west than the position initially described in the deed and on the chart.

The work crew charged with locating the Thomas Point lighthouse likely arrived at or near the prescribed location and then moved slowly and carefully around the end of the shoal, taking soundings and investigating the characteristics of the bottom. The location they selected is at the tip of the shoal, in about eight feet of water, where the top layer of the bottom is soft sand and mud, studded with oyster shells, that quickly turns into hard-packed sand. The bottom drops away quickly to forty feet below the surface just a few hundred yards east of the site.

Thomas Point Shoal Lighthouse stands at:

38 53' 56" North Latitude
76 26' 09" West Longitude

The material and men required to build Thomas Point Shoal Lighthouse traveled south from Baltimore, all likely aboard *Tulip*, the Lighthouse Board's steam-powered tender. They might have stopped at Annapolis and waited for an appropriate weather window. It is likely that smaller workboats accompanied *Tulip* to the site. Once the site was selected and marked, a staging barge was anchored in place, and the hard work began.

The first step at the lighthouse site was drilling the wrought-iron piles and their cast-iron screws into the Bay's bottom. Precision was key. Typically, the center pile was set first and a specially built jig was then fitted to the center pile and used to precisely measure the distance out to each of the six surrounding pilings. In the case of Thomas Point, the center of each surrounding piling was twenty-one feet from the center of the center piling. A hexagon was formed with sixty-degree angles at the center. The seven screwpiles at the central hexagon were augmented by additional pilings driven to the north and south of the central hexagon and designed as icebreakers. These pilings were tied back to the central hexagon.

Unfortunately, the exact manner of how the Thomas Point screwpiles were driven into the Bay bottom appears to be undocumented. However, twenty-five years earlier, the Delaware Bay screwpile lighthouse, America's first, was built with screws driven into the bottom of the Delaware Bay by thirty men working a four-foot-tall capstan. It is likely that this or a similar method was used at Thomas Point. An article in an 1878 engineering magazine stated, "A screw pile turned by eight capstan bars, twenty feet long, each moved by four or five men, with a screw four feet in diameter, passed in less than two hours through a stratum of sand and clay more than twenty feet thick, the surface of which was about twenty feet below water, and dug itself to a depth of about one foot into an underlying schistose rock."

In 1889, Ira Osborn Baker, writing in his *A Treatise on Masonry Construction*, noted, "These piles are usually screwed into the soil by men working with capstan bars…of course steam or horse power could be used for this purpose."

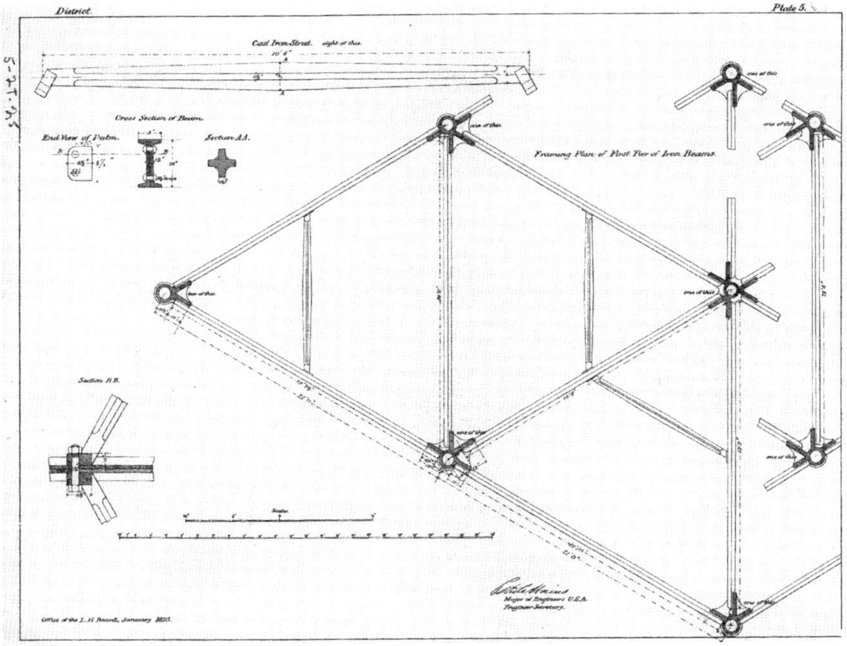

Detail of the framing of the iron beam infrastructure for the Thomas Point Shoal screwpile lighthouse, as illustrated in plans published by the U.S. Lighthouse Board in January 1875. *U.S. National Archives and Records Administration.*

It is likely that human or possibly steam power was used to drive the Thomas Point piles, although some local oral history in Annapolis holds that oxen or horses were barged out to the end of the shoal for the purpose of turning a capstan. It is documented that each of the nine pilings for the new lighthouse was driven eleven and a half feet into the Bay's bottom.

These piles were then tied together by beams bolted to the heads of the piles, about two feet above the average high tide. An additional pair of "outstanding piles"—icebreakers—were later drilled into the shoal, one north and one south of the main structure, and tied back into the foundation. A boarding platform was built just above the water level that could also be used to store fuel and, potentially, livestock.

The cottage attached atop the foundation is made of wood and shaped, like its base, as a hexagon, with each side measuring eighteen feet and having a diameter of thirty-five feet. The cottage is covered by wooden, horizontal lap siding, painted white. The main level is surrounded by a deck gallery (deck or porch), which is defined by a series of decorative wooden balusters. A privy hangs over the water off the south side of the main-level gallery. A

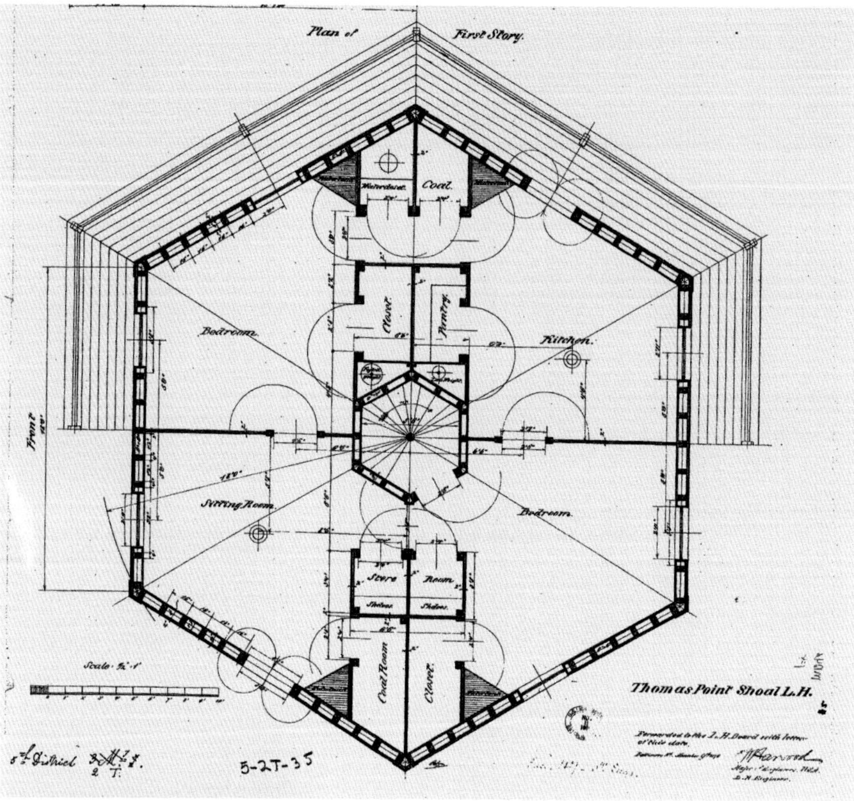

Above: Layout of the first story of the cottage at the Thomas Point Shoal screwpile lighthouse, as illustrated in plans published by the U.S. Lighthouse Board in January 1875. *U.S. National Archives and Records Administration.*

Left: Kit part markings, believed to be 1875 original, found by lighthouse preservation workers on beams behind the exterior cornice on the east side of the cottage. *Photo by John Potwin.*

smaller, second level was more open and features six distinctive dormers. The lantern level is ringed by a smaller but similar gallery as below, including the decorative balusters. A copper roof was installed atop the cottage; it was later replaced by red-painted sheet metal. No photos or press reports of the building of the lighthouse have been located.

AS CONSTRUCTION ON THE Thomas Point screwpile and the Currituck tower moved forward, Fifth District officials accelerated their campaign to mark and light various shoals and obstacles—aiming, as always, to complete an ambitious list before winter arrived. The spring and summer of 1875 saw the Fifth District pursue construction of a series of new lighthouses destined for points across the Virginia and the Maryland portions of the Bay. The second half of 1875 was especially busy. In early August, a more powerful light was installed at York Spit in Virginia. "The change has been highly appreciated by mariners," the lighthouse service later reported. The following week, a new screwpile was commissioned at Tue Marshes at the mouth of the York. Less than four weeks later, another new screwpile was lit at Solomon's Lump in Kedge's Straits, just north of Maryland's Smith Island. In North Carolina, the iconic Cape Hatteras Lighthouse was repaired and repainted. Nearby, a screwpile at Royal Shoal, North Carolina, was re-roofed and repaired.

By the end of 1875, the Fifth District would be responsible for no fewer than seventy-five lighthouses and nearly seven hundred buoys, across all corners of the district. The new Thomas Point screwpile, the last Chesapeake lighthouse built that year before winter arrived, and the new Currituck tower, the last Fifth District lighthouse completed in 1875, were included in the year-end tally.

ON NOVEMBER 15, WITH winter quickly approaching, the screwpile at Love Point, which marked the entrance to Maryland's Chester River, was downgraded from a 3½ Order Fresnel lens to a less powerful Fifth Order. The station at Love Point, while important enough to have a lighthouse, was not on the primary shipping lane to Baltimore. No direct link between the 3½ Order Fresnel lens removed from Love Point and the 3½ Order Fresnel lens installed five days later at Thomas Point Shoal has been found, but it is not illogical to make the connection. Fresnel lenses were treasured pieces of technology, and a working 3½ Order was a valuable asset. The new keeper at Thomas Point, Eugene Burchenal, had previously worked as an assistant at Love Point and kept that specific Fresnel lens before his new assignment. It is likely that both the new Thomas Point lens and keeper made the fourteen-mile trip from Love Point to Thomas Point, perhaps together aboard one of the Lighthouse Service tenders.

It is frequently reported that a Fourth Order Fresnel lens was installed at Thomas Point at its commissioning. The Lighthouse Board's 1876 annual report, as presented to Congress, stated that Thomas Point Shoal opened on November 20, 1875, with a 3½ Order lens. The information about the removal of the 3½ Order lens at nearby Love Point is also included in this report.

THE NEW LIGHTHOUSE ON the Thomas Point Shoal went into service in late November 1875 with minimal ceremony. The "Notice to Mariners" that announced the new station reported that the lighthouse was lit on November 20, and the shore tower was extinguished at the same time. To tend its new screwpile, the Lighthouse Board turned to thirty-five-year-old Eugene

Looking west at Thomas Point Shoal Lighthouse. The heavily wooded shape of Thomas Point itself is visible in the distance, just to the left of the lighthouse. *Photo by the author.*

Burchenal, a wounded veteran of the Civil War. Thomas Point would be Burchenal's first assignment as head keeper. Two men were assigned to assist him. Upon entering service, Thomas Point's kerosene-fueled lamp flashed red every twenty seconds. The light was reported to be visible for nearly twelve miles. When needed, and after being wound by a keeper, a one-thousand-pound, automated fog bell struck three times every thirty seconds.

THE 158-FOOT BRICK TOWER at Currituck, lit ten days after Thomas Point, was a triumph. As if to stamp an exclamation mark on the project, the Lighthouse Board installed a First Order Fresnel lens, standing nearly eight feet tall and weighing six tons, capable of projecting a light that could be seen eighteen miles offshore.

On December 18, 1875, less than a month after Thomas Point was lit, the *Baltimore Sun* ran a story titled "The Currituck Light-House—Its Advantage to Baltimore Commerce." The Thomas Point commissioning was scarcely mentioned.

The distinctive brick tower at Currituck Beach, North Carolina, long awaited by mariners and shipping interests, opened just a few weeks after the Thomas Point Shoal Lighthouse and received considerably more coverage in the Baltimore newspapers. *Photo by Carol M. Highsmith, Library of Congress.*

A short Thomas Point announcement did appear on page three of the December 4, 1875 edition of the *Annapolis Maryland Republican and State Capital Advertiser*, buried among news of railroads, canals and hunting accidents:

> *Eugene Burchenal took the oath of office yesterday, before Justice Wm. H. Gassaway, as principal light house keeper of Thomas' Point Shoal light, situated about a mile to the South-east of the old Light. The last named light house was dispensed with on the 20th.... The other officers of the Shoal Light House are—First Assistant—George E. Sullivan; Second Assistant—Charles Miller; Steward—James Ford.*

The same day, the *Baltimore Sun* mentioned the new lighthouse but focused on Miller and his connection to Baltimore. The item reads in its entirety:

> *Lighthouse Keeper—Capt. Chas. Miller, Sr. has been appointed assistant lighthouse keeper at Thomas's Point light, Chesapeake bay, and has entered upon duty. Captain Miller is a veteran Baltimore seaman, having at different times sailed vessels for leading shipowners in this port.*

On December 1, a sharp change in the weather blew through at Thomas Point, quickly dropping the temperature at Annapolis from forty-five degrees to nineteen degrees. In reporting the change, a local newspaper stated that "heavy wrappings and hot fires were the only comfortable things to be found. Ice of considerable thickness has formed every day since."

Burchenal, Miller, Sullivan and Ford would almost immediately see how the new lighthouse responded to ice, although the most extreme test was still a year away. The new lighthouse on the shoal also provided a front row to the heated battle over the valuable Chesapeake Bay oysters that lined the bottom at Thomas Point and nearby. As the new lighthouse was opened, a bold captain in Maryland's oyster police was sweeping across the middle Chesapeake, using unorthodox tactics and sailing with a sense of urgency that eventually led to the fatal shootings of two Baltimore oystermen.

LEMUEL MITCHELL AND THE OYSTER NAVY

When the oystermen can reap their bivalve harvest with as little trouble in the waters that are free as in the waters that are forbidden, it appears they do so… they invade the preserves against the peace and dignity of the people of Maryland.
—*"Poached Oysters,"* Harper's Weekly, *March 1, 1884*

In a fading November breeze, Captain Lemuel Mitchell led the Maryland Oyster Navy sloop *Nannie Merryman* up Eastern Bay into the heart of Maryland's Eastern Shore. A few years earlier, Maryland's General Assembly created an Oyster Navy with a goal of bringing order to the chaos of the Chesapeake Bay's booming oyster trade. On this afternoon, Lem Mitchell, although new to his position with the Oyster Navy, would put himself in the center of the action. Mitchell knew that his reception on the Shore would be cheered by some and cursed by more—this was the nature of the work. The entrance to the Miles River lay off his starboard bow, hidden behind a heavily wooded strip of land. When *Nannie* and its small crew were about a mile away, adjacent to the strip of wooded land, Mitchell stopped the sloop's forward progress and ordered the sails lowered and the anchor set. Mitchell knew that his plan was simple, but sometimes the simplest plans are the best—especially with boats, guns, hot tempers and money in the mix.

The Miles River extends south and east from Eastern Bay—its shoreline defined by rich woodlands, profitable farms and a few imposing estates—but the real treasure lay beneath its surface. In the fall of 1873, as Mitchell approached the Miles, acres of oysters spread across the river bottom. By law, these valuable Miles River oyster bars were reserved for hand-tongers, the local oystermen who harvested slowly, on a small scale, from the edges of small boats. This was dangerous, back-wrenching work, but a diligent tongs-man could scrape together a living on the water, as long as the oysters were present. The greatest threat to the tongs-men's livelihood, and the entire Miles River oyster population, were the Baltimore schooners. A fleet of these schooners, Mitchell suspected, was currently on the river dredging up more oysters with a single "lick" of the bottom than a tongs-man could gather in a full day.

A Chesapeake Bay oyster tonger working from the side of his small boat in 1905. Although this image was captured in the twentieth century, the methodology and equipment had remained unchanged for decades prior to this scene. *Library of Congress.*

The oyster schooners and their dredging equipment were, by law, forbidden from operating on the Miles, but demand for oysters in Baltimore had moved prices higher. An enterprising schooner captain could enjoy a few illegal sessions on the Miles and then fall back into the open Chesapeake, where he was permitted to dredge, with a hold already packed with river oysters. By the letter of the law, these men were poachers, but Maryland newspapers and national magazines often called them "pirates." Captain Lemuel Mitchell and the crew of the *Nannie Merryman* were tasked with rooting out and stopping the pirate dredging. The Baltimore men might not yet know Mitchell's name, but they knew *Nannie* and they knew that the Oyster Navy could arrive at any point. At the first sight of the police sloop, the schooner's gear would be hauled back aboard. Mitchell wanted to catch them in the act.

With the narrow strip of land at Tilghman Point serving as cover for his anchored sloop, Mitchell ordered a man to row to the point in *Nannie*'s yawl boat, a small tender that traveled with the *Nannie*. After beaching the boat, the man walked a few hundred feet through the woods and was soon on the edge of the Miles River with a sweeping view of the oyster bars and more than a dozen schooners working over them. A few minutes later, the breathless man was back aboard *Nannie*, where the sails were up and drawing even as the anchor line piled up wet on the deck. Captain Mitchell wasn't exactly sure what might happen next, but he had the authority to arrest men and boats; he carried a gun in case things got heated. Another, larger gun was mounted on *Nannie*'s bow.

As Lemuel Mitchell suspected, the schooners' dredging gear came out of the water as soon as the Baltimore crews spotted *Nannie Merryman* rounding Tilghman Point. Even as the crews secured the dredges on deck, the schooners, under tow by men rowing yawl boats, beelined for an anchorage in a creek just inside the point. Mitchell followed. Captain Mitchell and the crew of the *Nannie Merryman* heard the jeers as they entered the anchorage. He counted seventeen schooners and pungies anchored and rafted together, with sails furled and crews lounging on deck as if they were simply waiting out a change in the weather. The captains claimed innocence, but when Lemuel Mitchell boarded the schooners, he found wet decks, wet lines and piles of freshly caught oysters. He immediately put the captains and crews under arrest and sent them into nearby St. Michaels.

In the 1870s, St. Michaels was a rough waterman's outpost, but its magistrate and residents had little patience for Baltimore watermen illegally depleting the local oyster beds. Angered by the unplanned detour into St.

Michaels, the pirate oystermen vocally protested. As he heard the cases, the St. Michaels magistrate was forced to stop several times and fine the Baltimore men, who used profane language in his office. A group of ship captains asked to travel to Easton, where they could telegraph the bad news to their ships' owners back in Baltimore. Two of these poachers were arrested for disorderly conduct and put in the Easton jail. Back at St. Michaels, ten captains were fined $200 each. One was fined $100. One was acquitted. Five were held for further examination.

In a single operation, Captain Lemuel Mitchell had halted a major poaching operation and forced seventeen captains to account for their actions. In its next edition, the *Maryland Republican* newspaper was effusive in its praise for the new officer's effort:

> *Miles River has swarmed with dredging vessels all the season. A few more raids like this of Captain Mitchell's will effectively check it; and unless it is checked soon the oyster beds of Miles River, upon which several hundred tongsmen depend for a living, will be broken. Many beds are now so depleted that they can no longer be worked with profit by the tongs-men.*

While the Miles River locals and the conservation-minded politicians and editorial writers on the western shore were thrilled with Mitchell's work, his aggressiveness and success was generally unpopular along the Baltimore waterfront, where thousands were employed in the oyster business. Shortly after the Miles River raid, a group representing the oyster industry traveled to Annapolis and appeared before the Board of State Fishing Force. It complained about Captain Mitchell's aggressive actions. The board, chaired by Maryland's governor, patiently listened to the complaints and moved to pacify the Baltimore oystermen. Captain Mitchell was instructed that he had no authority under the law to take licenses from dredgers and that he was to return any in his possession. The board also reminded Captain Mitchell that while he was to bring to trial all violators of the law, he was to exercise discretion in the enforcement of the law and should conduct himself with calmness and moderation when making arrests. The board ordered Mitchell to begin keeping a notebook and to log information about the law-breaking boats and licenses he encountered. Despite the reprimand and the expanded new procedures, Mitchell and the members of the oyster industry were all reminded that Mitchell and his mission had real backing in Annapolis. "If they will not come into trial at the order of the captain," the board noted, "then the steamer will enforce this part of the law."

After the board meeting, Lemuel Mitchell returned to the water as news of his bold operation spread. He had served notice and seemed to have the weight of the state behind him, for now. In Baltimore, where schooners and operating cash were provided by syndicates and wealthy owners intent on profiting from the booming the oyster business, Lem Mitchell's name was now met with frowns and grumbles on wharves, in counting houses, in darkened pubs and in the modest parlors of working-class East Baltimore. Mitchell knew that the next time he encountered Baltimore oystermen on the Bay, they would likely come at him with more than jeers and profanity.

ONE OF EIGHT CHILDREN, Lemuel Jefferson Mitchell was born in 1834. He spent his early childhood in Havre de Grace, Maryland, where his father worked on the water. In the 1850s, the Mitchell family moved south to Annapolis. At the dawn of the 1860s, twenty-six-year-old Lemuel Mitchell listed his occupation as a painter, although it is likely he also fished and worked on the water off Annapolis. On the first day of the new decade, he married nineteen-year-old Rachel Stewart, and the couple stayed together more than fifty years.

Lem enlisted in the U.S. Army in 1862 and served as a private with Maryland's First Regiment through his discharge in 1864. In 1870, he and Rachel lived in Annapolis with their two young sons, and Mitchell worked as carpenter. The events of the following decade proved that Lemuel Mitchell was, by this point, far more than a simple painter or carpenter. He had acquired the skills of a Chesapeake Bay waterman and the trust of the state government.

The operations of Maryland's Oyster Navy were nuanced, complicated and often dangerous. Baltimore commercial interests were fueled by muscle, flowing cash and the city's powerful political machine. The interests of the Baltimore industry were often in direct opposition to those of conservation-minded state officials and those of small-scale, local tongers and hamlets along the Bay. The political will to maximize or carefully manage the oyster harvest ebbed and flowed in the political halls of Annapolis.

As market demand for oysters surged, along with prices, four cornerstone laws governed the fishery:

- No dredges in rivers; the rivers are reserved for tongers. This would protect local watermen and would also slow the depletion of oyster beds.

- No out-of-state boats oystering in Maryland waters.
- No dredging at night.
- No oystering on Sunday.

Despite the Oyster Navy's efforts, all four of these laws were broken regularly.

By 1871, despite the presence of the Oyster Navy, dredge boats frequently moved, en masse, into the prohibited rivers of the Chesapeake, where they collected oysters in an ever more efficient process. To combat the poaching, the state brought new recruits into the Oyster Navy force. Lemuel Mitchell, based at Annapolis, was among the recruits.

Much of his work was in the waters near Annapolis, but Mitchell ranged across the Chesapeake as needed. Less than two months after the Miles River Raid, on January 2, 1874, Mitchell and the *Nannie Merryman* captured a pair of Baltimore schooners that had been dredging illegally at Hollands Island Bar, more than sixty miles south of Annapolis. Both captains were sent to jail.

Unloading the oyster boats with wicker bushel baskets and horse-drawn carts at Baltimore, circa 1905. *Library of Congress.*

Reports of the nineteenth-century Oyster Wars on the Chesapeake Bay captured the imagination of the public, and the magazines and newspapers of the day responded with extensive coverage. A Schell and Hogan wood engraving evocatively captioned "Pirates dredging at night" appeared in the March 1, 1884 edition of *Harper's Weekly*. *Library of Congress.*

One month later, at Thomas Point, Mitchell spotted a Baltimore pungy illegally dredging. As the *Merryman* approached, the poacher's crew raised all its sails and took off in order to avoid capture. With *Merryman* in pursuit, the pungy crossed the Bay. At the southern tip of Kent Island, a towboat friendly to the poachers appeared and took the pungy under tow. Mitchell and *Merryman* pursued the towboat and poacher south and finally captured the pungy. The captain was taken to a judge at Solomons Island and fined fifty dollars.

In early November 1874, Mitchell found the Baltimore schooner *Corelia C* dredging illegally at Hollands Island Bar. As a result, the schooner was chained to the dock at Annapolis and the captain sent to jail. A few weeks later, back at Hollands Island Bar, Mitchell captured *Speed*, another Baltimore schooner. After securing *Speed*, Captain Mitchell gave chase to a pair of vessels that had also been dredging on the bar. In the chase, Mitchell fired four two-pounder balls from the cannon on *Nannie*'s bow; one of the shots fell very near a pirate vessel, while another shot passed through the vessel's sails. After a chase of ten miles at Cove Point, Mitchell gave up the chase; however, as an Annapolis newspaper reported, "He knows one of the vessels and will be able hereafter to capture it."

By early 1875, as planning for the new lighthouse at Thomas Point Shoal was underway, Annapolis judges began setting bail for captains guilty of poaching as high as $500, which further raised the stakes in the cat-and-mouse game between oyster poachers and the Maryland Oyster Navy.

In late February 1875, Lemuel Mitchell was ashore in Annapolis serving as a witness in an illegal dredging trial. As the trial took place, six defiant schooners set sail from the city's piers. At the conclusion of the trial, Mitchell and crew boarded *Nannie Merryman* and headed out into the Chesapeake, certain that the six planned to dredge on prohibited grounds. The Three Sisters, a series of low-lying islands just a few miles south of Thomas Point (they are now submerged), had become a popular place for poachers, and Mitchell suspected this was the destination.

Nannie's pursuit was later reported in an Annapolis newspaper: "The *Merryman* hugged the shore as close as possible to keep out of sight of the schooners and rounded Tally's Point so near the shore that the sand grated on the keel all the way."

Mitchell reached Thomas Point in late afternoon and, using the point itself as cover, anchored and sent a small boat ashore to reconnoiter. Once ashore, a member of Mitchell's crew walked across the point and spotted one schooner aground on the Three Sisters Island bar and a pair anchored at the bar. With night quickly approaching, one of the schooners anchored a small boat on the bar with a light fixed aboard to serve as a reference point for the dredgers.

Upon nightfall, the two anchored schooners got underway and began to illegally dredge. In a southerly wind, Mitchell moved toward the schooners, which quickly tacked away in an effort to escape. The *Maryland Republican* newspaper later recounted the events on its front page and under the heading "An Exciting Capture." The article stated, "The *Merryman* passed so close…a man could have jumped aboard, but for fear of hurting the man among the oyster shell, Captain Mitchell did not give the order. The dredger hauled to and Captain Mitchell sent a prize crew aboard the schooner, which proved to be the *Romer*."

Mitchell then turned his attention to the other schooner, the *Harper*, which had by this time hauled in its dredges and was pushing north, up the Bay. Darkness had fallen, and according to the newspaper account, "the stars [were] giving light enough for steering purposes."

As the chase began, *Harper* floated about three hundred yards ahead of the *Nannie*. As *Harper* fled, Mitchell and his crew manned the gun on *Nannie*'s bow and "poured into the fugitive round after round, as fast as they could

The March 1, 1884 issue of *Harper's Weekly* featured this illustration of "The pirates attacking the police schooner *Julia Hamilton*," a scene that mirrors Lemuel Mitchell's earlier experiences on Thomas Point Shoal. *Library of Congress.*

load and fire." Over the course of a half hour, more than one hundred one-ounce balls were fired at *Harper*. During this time, *Nannie* closed to within fifty yards of the schooner. Captain Mitchell ran forward and hailed the fleeing schooner. Badly damaged, it was hove-to at Mitchell's request. *Nannie*'s assault had cut *Harper*'s rigging, damaged its mast and blown holes through its sails. The captain later told Mitchell that he would stay at the helm until he saw the flash of *Nannie*'s gun, and then he would duck into the safety of his cabin. The newspaper reported that the poacher "had run up and down the companionway so many times that he became so stiff he could hardly walk."

Upon their return to Annapolis, both captains pled guilty to dredging at night and were fined $150 each, a relatively light penalty. Annapolis residents devoured news of such captures, complete with gunfire just a few miles from their homes.

As the winter unfolded, additional prizes were taken by Mitchell and his crew aboard *Nannie*, including captures of Baltimore-based poachers at the Three Sisters and in Poplar Island Narrows. In May 1875, as the parts of the new Thomas Point screwpile were being fabricated, seven crews were brought to court simultaneously for violating oyster laws. So thorough was Mitchell's pursuit and reporting that all seven pled guilty without Mitchell even needing to testify. The *Maryland Republican* newspaper gushed, "Anne Arundel seems to have the champion capturer of dredgers."

That same month, Mitchell purchased a lot in Eastport, across Spa Creek from the Annapolis city dock. The lot was directly on the creek, near the wooden bridge connecting Annapolis and Eastport. Mitchell planned to build a home on it and proposed to fill in sixty feet of waterfront to construct a modern wharf that, according to a newspaper account, would be the first on the Eastport peninsula.

The 1875 oyster season started in the usual fashion. Baltimore-based boats continued to test the limits of the Oyster Navy's authority, and Mitchell continued his hot pursuit. By late November, he had already captured thirteen vessels, primarily Baltimore dredgers that had come to the Annapolis area and its lucrative oyster beds. "Captain Lemuel Mitchell is still after the dredgers with a sharp stick," the *Maryland Republican* reported.

JUST A FEW DAYS after the new Thomas Point Shoal screwpile opened, its keepers witnessed an extraordinary set of events involving Lemuel Mitchell. On Friday, November 26, Mitchell had what an Annapolis newspaper called "quite a lively skirmish with dredgers." Having been informed that illegal dredging was taking place at the Three Sisters area, only a few miles south of Thomas Point, Mitchell descended on the scene. Several of the poachers attempted to flee, and Mitchell responded with a hail of gunfire from *Nannie*'s bow. An estimated two hundred shots were fired. Three pirate captains were arrested for illegally dredging, and a fourth escaped, frantically rowing away in his pungy's yawl boat.

On Thursday, December 9, Mitchell captured a schooner named *Kent Island* and brought it to Annapolis. Relying on his cleverness and the slow spread of information over the waters, Mitchell assembled a group of sixteen "firm and reliable" men. For this trip, Mitchell had left the familiar *Nannie Merryman* at the dock in Annapolis and led his crew into the Chesapeake aboard the captured schooner on the evening of Friday, December 10. Mitchell and crew sailed past the new lighthouse and continued south, spending the night in the vicinity of the Three Sisters alongside several other dredge boats. At dawn on Saturday morning, Mitchell's men stood at the dredges of their captured schooner and went through the motions of preparing for a dredging session.

A Frank Cresson illustration depicting "An engagement in the oyster war on the Chesapeake" appeared in the January 9, 1886 edition of *Harper's Weekly*. It shows a police steamer engaged with several oyster schooners. *Library of Congress.*

Believing that they were in the friendly company of fellow watermen, seven nearby vessels hoisted sail and began illegally dredging Hollands Island Bar. Mitchell quickly moved into action and arrested six ship captains. Several shots were exchanged in the process. When they returned to Annapolis, three of the captains, perhaps repeat offenders or surly prisoners, had their bail set at $1,000 each. The ensuing newspaper headline was straightforward: "The Oyster War—Wholesale Arrests."

THE FIRST KEEPER ON THE SHOAL

Although the pay is small and the life often lonely, the work of the Lighthouse Service attracts as a rule an excellent class of faithful men, willing to take large risks in doing their duty, and helping others in distress.
—George Rockwell Putnam, commissioner of lighthouses, 1910–35

Abraham Lincoln spent the first few months of his presidency making repeated calls for additional volunteers to join the U.S. Army in anticipation of a coming conflict that he, and most others, saw as inevitable. Predictably, the southern states pushed back against Lincoln, and not long after Lincoln's inauguration, the smoldering American Civil War sparked into a hot conflict. A special session of Congress met on July 4, 1861, and following an impassioned speech from Lincoln, a call for 500,000 new soldiers was authorized.

A few weeks later, twenty-year-old Eugene Burchenal arrived at Wilmington, Delaware, where the First Delaware Infantry Regiment was re-forming and preparing to move south onto Confederate soil. Standing five-foot-ten with dark hair and blue eyes, the young Burchenal committed for a three-year term. Eugene Burchenal was born in Caroline County, Maryland's only landlocked Eastern Shore county. He grown up in Smyrna, a small central Delaware town about thirty miles south of Wilmington. At Smyrna, Burchenal served an apprenticeship with a coach maker and, at the time of his enlistment in the First Delaware, declared his occupation as "Harness Maker."

With no apparent experience and a limited formal education, Eugene Burchenal was made a private and assigned to Company G. He turned twenty-one during the initial weeks of training at Wilmington and, in mid-October, was among the 846 enlisted infantry men who moved south into Virginia with the First Delaware. This was likely the first time he had ever been outside Maryland and Delaware.

Eugene Burchenal and his compatriots spent their first winter together at Camp Hamilton in Hampton, Virginia. Camp Hamilton was the first U.S. Army base established on Southern soil after the states' secession and remained surrounded by a strong Rebel population. Predictably, the spring of 1862 brought action in and around nearby Norfolk. In early May, President Lincoln visited the area and contributed to the strategic planning process, and soon afterward, the emboldened Union established an occupation at Norfolk. Private Burchenal and the First Delaware spent a tense summer defending this occupation.

In early September, with Norfolk under martial law, Eugene Burchenal and the First Delaware moved north to Washington, D.C., and, from there, northwest into rural Maryland. After a fifty-five-mile march, they reached a stretch of farmland framed by the Blue Ridge Mountains to the east and the upper Potomac River to the west. Private Burchenal didn't know it yet, but he was among more than 125,000 Union and Confederate soldiers converging on this bucolic spot.

On the morning of September 17, 1862, Eugene Burchenal and the First Delaware regiment crossed Antietam Creek and formed up on the right side of the Union line alongside a regiment out of Baltimore. They faced southwest on the edge of a rolling, open field. Across the field were an unknown number of Confederate soldiers who coyly moved forward using a worn and low-lying farm road as cover. From there, the Rebels began moving into the field toward the Union line.

Around 9:15 a.m., Private Burchenal, the First Delaware and the Maryland regiment moved forward through the open field and engaged in heavy skirmishing. In the course of a fierce exchange, the First Delaware and other Union forces successfully pushed the Rebels back toward the sunken road, establishing a high-ground position for themselves in the process. But even as the Union soldiers made forward progress, they moved directly into the heart of a Confederate division. Burchenal and his compatriots were soon greatly outmanned and outgunned.

Despite the long odds, Eugene Burchenal and the men of the First Delaware bravely engaged in intense fighting at and near Antietam's infamous sunken road. In this action, eight of the 10 Delaware Company commanders were killed or wounded, as was the entire 9-man color guard. By sunset, more than 22,000 men were dead, wounded or missing, and the day was soon called the bloodiest in American history. Counted among the dead were 3 Delaware officers and 26 men; 10 of the regiment's officers and 172 men had been wounded. Among the wounded at Antietam was Private Eugene Burchenal, struck by two musket balls and wounded in the head by a shell. The shell wound resulted in a head fracture. One of the musket balls entered his left shoulder and was later extracted from his left arm. A second musket ball passed through his left hip into his left groin. A surgeon later extracted the ball and ten pieces of bone.

Eugene Burchenal was sent to recover at the U.S. Army General Hospital No. 1 at Frederick, Maryland, and then the army hospital at Wilmington. Following that, he was moved to a hospital in Washington, where, in October 1863, Burchenal's disability was declared "total." He was discharged from the army, awarded a pension of four dollars per month and moved back to Smyrna. He didn't stay there long. On July 11, 1864, with the Civil War still raging, Burchenal reenlisted and served a short period, despite his disability.

The following spring, he reenlisted again, this time with the U.S. Veteran Volunteers. His third enlistment lasted more than a year, and the Confederates surrendered during this term of service. Eugene Burchenal was discharged at Philadelphia on April 17, 1866.

By 1867, Eugene Burchenal was a twenty-seven-year-old wounded veteran on the winning side of the war. Records show him working as a saddle and harness maker in the quiet Eastern Shore hamlet of Queenstown, Maryland, on the Chester River.

In the months after the Civil War, the strategically positioned Chesapeake Bay again became central to the American economy. Consequently, the Bay's network of navigational aids, including manned lighthouses, expanded. The keeper corps grew simultaneously. Sandy Clunies, past historian of the Chesapeake chapter of the U.S. Lighthouse Society, noted that the process of selecting new lighthouse keepers was now managed in Washington by the Lighthouse Board, although recommendations from local sources, such as other keepers and mariners, were collected. Clunies said, "In those first decades after the Civil War, the federal government valued Union veterans—they were loyal citizens to the Union." Eugene Burchenal, carrying an unassailable record of loyalty and action in the name of duty, entered the service. A screwpile, rather than a tall tower with many steps, made sense for Burchenal, who was likely limited in mobility. In October 1873, he was appointed first assistant at the new Love Point screwpile lighthouse at the mouth of the Chester River, less than ten miles northwest of Queenstown.

At the time of Burchenal's arrival at Love Point, the station was just three years old. The new open-water screwpile design was unproven and vulnerable to ice floes and damage from wayward ships and flotsam. In its first winter, prior to Burchenal's arrival, the Love Point station had been tested by ice, and the screwpile had been damaged in an incident that saw its keepers abandon the screwpile in fear that it would be carried away. The subsequent investigation determined that the keepers had left their station earlier than deemed appropriate. They were found to be guilty of desertion and dismissed from the Lighthouse Service. Keeping an open-water screwpile was already a risky business, but the overhanging fear of having one's emergency decisions later judged and possibly punished by distant officials only added to the tension. Eugene Burchenal appears to have done his first assistant keeper job well. He was soon a candidate for a new, high-profile assignment.

TO THE SOUTH OF Love Point, the new Thomas Point Shoal screwpile station would also be vulnerable to ice floes, likely even more than Love Point. The new station was out at the end of a shoal, nearly in the center of the open Chesapeake. Nonetheless, given its important position on the Baltimore shipping route and its proximity to pleasant Annapolis, Thomas Point was likely considered to be a choice assignment.

In 1875, as the offshore Thomas Point station was under construction, the old Thomas Point shore tower was kept by George Sullivan, a twenty-five-year-old father of three. Sullivan had taken over the tower keeper role from his father-in-law, John Wayson, in July 1874. Sullivan had tended the stone tower for more than a year, but when it was time to choose a permanent keeper for its newest screwpile, the Lighthouse Service turned to Eugene Burchenal. George Sullivan would serve as first assistant keeper, a demotion. Newcomer Charles Miller came aboard as second assistant. A steward named James Ford rounded out the team.

Despite the potential for tension between the newcomer Burchenal, the rookie keeper Miller and Sullivan, the passed-over local, the three appear to have developed a solid working relationship. No significant incidents at the light have been found reported in the first months of operation. The new light burned brightly, shipping traffic flowed past and the rotation on and off the station continued. What might have happened or been said behind the scenes in those early months aboard the screwpile is lost to history.

The new lighthouse and the relationships between its keepers would soon be harshly tested.

THE ICE EMERGENCY

With demand for oysters at historic highs, more than a thousand schooners and pungies set out to be part of the 1876–77 Chesapeake Bay oyster season. Baltimore's streets were paved with oyster shells, and its oyster canning industry employed thousands. New York's Fulton Fish Market could sell about fifty thousand oysters each day, many of which were delivered daily directly from Baltimore aboard trains. Oystermen were a rugged lot and diligently took to the Bay even when challenged by extended periods of winter weather. In early December 1876, a "polar hurricane" led to the stranding of five oyster schooners in the Chester River. According to the *Baltimore Sun*, "a number of lives were lost." The *Sun* continued, "The tale of suffering from freezing, starvation, and other privations would fill a volume." But those who could harvest oysters and safely return to port stood to make a handsome profit.

Several stretches of cold weather in early January 1877 froze the Bay solid and prevented most oystermen from leaving shore. With supply pinched, the price of oysters soared, ensuring a fat profit for those who were able to harvest any amount of oysters and get them back to shore. Many of those who ventured out into the cold waters were trapped when the Bay froze solid. Despite continuous efforts of boats repurposed for icebreaking duties, the Port of Baltimore had to impose an ice embargo on December 10—no major ship traffic could move in or out of the port.

On January 8, the approach to the harbor was finally clear enough for the embargo to be lifted. But the freezing temperatures soon returned, even colder than before, and the embargo was reinstated after just one open day. Among those stuck at Baltimore were the crew of *Lake Megantic*, a massive steamship with sixty-two thousand bushels of corn and fifty-five tons of oil cake in its holds, aiming for England but held prisoners by the Chesapeake ice.

At Annapolis, where the passage from the open Bay to a relatively safe anchorage stayed open longer and more consistently than in Baltimore, three hundred to five hundred vessels were trapped by the ice, unable to move on the Bay and on to Baltimore. Barques, brigs, schooners and pungies anchored en masse across the mouth of the Severn River, among them *Madcap*, a Baltimore-bound barque loaded with coffee, prevented by the ice from completing its passage. The majority of the ships were foreign, including vessels from Italy, Norway, Austria, Russia and England. Five large steamships waited at Annapolis for permission to move to Baltimore. The *Baltimore Sun* reported, "From Greenbury Point to Annapolis, a distance of three miles, the vessels were so thickly strung that one could walk from deck to deck to the city. On entering the harbor from the Bay the dense forest of masts almost obscured the ancient city from view." The *Maryland Republican* newspaper of Annapolis reported:

> *When it was impossible for the hundreds of tugboats, steamers, ice boats, and other boats to keep the Patapsco River open sufficiently to allow an unimpeded commerce to the city of Baltimore, our harbor always presented an opening in the ice broad enough for the largest vessels to secure a passage to the wharves of the city…numerous coasters came to our haven to seek shelter from the unimpeded blasts of winter and the death-bearing ice of the Chesapeake.*

Despite the freeze, a few ships were able to move; an icebreaker and small tugboats struggled around the clock in an effort to keep the shipping lanes open. Oystermen, desperate to work and propelled by the high prices offered for any oyster catch—the price of a bushel of oysters had quickly doubled—somehow found a way to leave the docks.

The *Maryland Republican* newspaper of Annapolis reported, "The oyster dredges fear not the minions of the law just now and dredge on Sundays and on bars with the utmost impunity….The oyster police force are powerless to help the matter for the ice prevents them from making incursions on the depredators."

In a briefly clear weather window, the oyster schooner *Virginia* sailed from Annapolis under the command of Captain George Dobbins. Dobbins and his small crew aimed to collect Thomas Point oysters and return to shore before any heavier ice formed. Out on the Bay, the ice sliced at *Virginia*'s wooden hull, and the crew did not return to Annapolis as scheduled. On January 15, the *Baltimore Sun* reported from Annapolis, "A report prevails that the schooner *Virginia* of this place…has been cut through by ice and lost….The parties left here Sunday night week with the avowed object of getting a load of Thomas's Point oysters."

The boats that did make it back to the dock arrived bearing men suffering from frostbite, malnutrition and exhaustion. These men told shocking stories of hardship, but the demand for oysters remained incessant.

On the Eastern Bay, across the Chesapeake from Annapolis, about ninety oyster boats were locked in by the ice. Oyster vessels typically set out with about two weeks of provisions aboard, but many of these boats had already been away from port for more than three weeks. Their collective crews, estimated in newspapers at "not less than five hundred" men, had grown hungry, cold and impatient. Many stepped off their boats and onto the ice, eyes turned to the shore in desperation. One group of six crossed the ice, reached the shore and began walking home to Baltimore. They followed the coastline north, along the edge of the Eastern Shore, to Swan Point, where they found shelter in an old fish house. The following day, they crossed the frozen Bay on foot and were taken in by the keeper of the stone tower lighthouse at Pooles Island. Shortly after sunrise the following day, they reached the western shore and found a set of railroad tracks, which they followed into the city of Baltimore. Their walk home was eighty miles.

Other groups made their way back to Baltimore by similar means, arriving, as the *Sun* noted, "as tramps in squads, after untold sufferings, crowding the station-houses and hospitals, often with frozen extremities, thinly-clad, penniless, sick and without resources. Nothing could have been more pitiable than the evidence of extreme suffering presented by some off these previously strong men broken down in a few weeks by their Bay experiences."

As the ice began to break up in the middle of January, the oystermen who had been stuck ashore were desperate to get back to work and take advantage of the imbalance between oyster supply and demand. The conditions were still cold and dangerous, temperatures were below freezing and snow fell for several days after the ice broke up.

Lemuel Mitchell, aware that poachers would use any break in the weather to get back in business, traveled from Annapolis to Thomas Point, where he took note of several vessels illegally dredging.

This drawing, featuring tongers in rough waters, is from a collection of sketches by Joseph Becker titled "Gathering Oysters in the Great Beds in Chesapeake Bay, near Annapolis" and was captioned "Gathering and dredging oysters under difficulties" when it appeared in *Frank Leslie's Illustrated Newspaper* on February 8, 1879. *Library of Congress.*

Two weeks after the *Virginia* left Annapolis and after being assumed lost, news of the schooner reached Annapolis. It had been among the fleet in the Eastern Bay and had tangled with the Oyster Navy. *Virginia* and its crew were safe, but its captain was locked in the Easton jail, charged with dredging on prohibited ground.

On January 21, the typical Sunday quiet in Maryland's capital city was upset when nearly two dozen oystermen were unloaded onto a Spa Creek wharf. The men had been arrested for working on the Sabbath. They were formed into a straggling line and led up Compromise Street toward the magistrate's office for trial. By the time the line got to Main Street, several hundred curious townspeople had gathered to have a look at the prisoners. As the group moved up Main Street, one of the dredgers broke rank and darted into an alley. A police deputy shot at the fleeing man, but the ball struck the German Lutheran church. The crowd scattered in panic. The runaway dredger turned up Francis Street, where another deputy shot at the man—this ball entered the window frame of a drugstore. The runaway was finally chased down by a third deputy, who secured him at gunpoint. The group was reassembled and placed in the city jail.

The Annapolis newspaper reporter covering the story finished his piece with an admonishment: "[I]t may be said that the citizens generally disapprove of the reckless fusillade, as the lives and limbs of many persons were endangered. They would much prefer that such a prisoner should escape than the lives of others or the dredgers be imperiled."

"Light House Trouble"

Hooper Strait Lighthouse, a screwpile just off the Eastern Shore and forty-five miles southeast of Annapolis, was severely damaged by ice floes on January 11, 1877. As its base was attacked by ice, its cottage toppled into the Bay and floated southward with the ice floe. The runaway cottage was located several days later more than four miles from its original position. The lens, lantern, fog bell and some furniture were recovered. The Lighthouse Board immediately dispatched two vessels from Norfolk to locate the keepers, John Cornwell and Alexander Conway, who were still missing.

Cornwell and Conway later reported that as the cottage broke away from its foundation, they managed to escape danger by pulling one of the station's tenders across the frozen ice. They then made their way to a small island, where they waited with the boat, exposed to the elements, for twenty-four hours. Both were suffering from frostbite when a local rescue party arrived.

The men recovered slowly on a remote stretch of the Eastern Shore but had no means of communicating with their supervisors or the western shore. The lack of communication and the extreme conditions led the public to fear the worst. Newspapers began reporting on the missing keepers. On January 15, the *Baltimore Sun* reported, "It is the impression of the lighthouse authorities in Baltimore that neither has a family."

It took two weeks for Cornwell and Conway to reach a telegram station and alert the Lighthouse Board of their survival. Despite his ordeal, John Cornwell remained firm in his commitment to the Lighthouse Service. He wrote, "Should there be another house erected, or a boat placed on the site of the old one, Capt. Conway and myself will be ready to take charge of it."

While its structure was somewhat more reinforced than the screwpile at Hooper Strait, the Thomas Point screwpile stood in open waters near the center of the Chesapeake, in a position far more exposed to the main artery of the ice floe. Its keepers also faced a severe test.

BY SUNDAY, JANUARY 14, the ice had broken up to the point of allowing some passage through the Bay. The Bay came alive with ship traffic. Forty loaded vessels arrived in Baltimore behind tugs. An icebreaker led *Madcap*, the overdue coffee barque, through the last miles of its passage to Baltimore. On the following day, *Lake Megantic* passed Thomas Point en route from Baltimore to Liverpool, riding heavy with holds full of corn and oil cake.

Out at the end of the Thomas Point Shoal aboard the screwpile, Keeper Eugene Burchenal and his assistant, Charles Miller, felt the warming of the air and could see and hear the ice breaking up around the station. Their lamp would be more important than ever. The ships that had been blockaded in Baltimore, Annapolis and throughout the region would be looking for and depending on the Thomas Point Light.

Captain Miller's wife and their teenage son, George, were also aboard the station with the keepers, but First Assistant George Sullivan, the last keeper of the shore tower and the man who had been demoted when Burchenal arrived to lead the team at the new shoal screwpile, was absent. Miller, a family man, with four children and a home on Fleet Street in downtown Annapolis, had apparently been absent from his lighthouse responsibilities for some time prior to the ice emergency.

As the air warmed and a steady northwesterly wind blew in, the ice began moving, predominantly in a direction from north to south. Heavy ice slammed against the Thomas Point screwpile base, constantly vibrating the structure and producing sounds ranging from snapping like a small fire of dry twigs to very large bangs. As the piles and beams beneath it were shifted by the relentless ice floe, the cottage began to lean over. Burchenal and the Millers feverishly worked to stabilize the equipment inside the cottage. The stove was lashed down to keep it from falling over and spilling hot coals. Containers of lamp fuel turned over and spilled noxious liquid across the cottage floor. The angle of lean increased, and the clapper of the station's fog bell lay useless on the side of the bell. The *Baltimore Sun* ran a paragraph describing the situation at Thomas Point under the headline "Light House Trouble."

On Tuesday, January 16, the fourth day of the siege, the vibration and crashing grew so strong that the station's Fresnel lens, weighing upward of five hundred pounds, fell off its base and was damaged. Undeterred and aware of their duty as keepers, Burchenal and Charles Miller rigged a replacement light in a window.

The ice kept coming down the Bay. Having done all they could to stabilize the equipment and keep a light burning, the keepers discussed

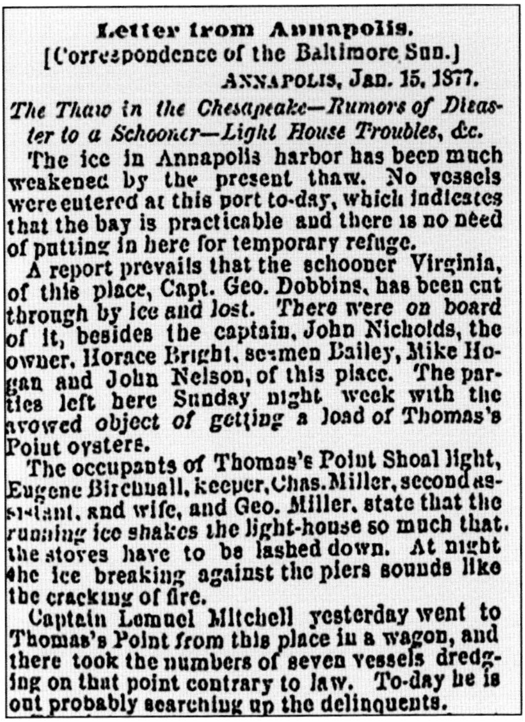

Letter from Annapolis.
[Correspondence of the Baltimore Sun.]
ANNAPOLIS, Jan. 15, 1877.

The Thaw in the Chesapeake—Rumors of Disaster to a Schooner—Light House Troubles, &c.

The ice in Annapolis harbor has been much weakened by the present thaw. No vessels were entered at this port to-day, which indicates that the bay is practicable and there is no need of putting in here for temporary refuge.

A report prevails that the schooner Virginia, of this place, Capt. Geo. Dobbins, has been cut through by ice and lost. There were on board of it, besides the captain, John Nicholds, the owner, Horace Bright, seamen Bailey, Mike Hogan and John Nelson, of this place. The parties left here Sunday night week with the avowed object of getting a load of Thomas's Point oysters.

The occupants of Thomas's Point Shoal light, Eugene Birchnall, keeper, Chas. Miller, second assistant, and wife, and Geo. Miller, state that the running ice shakes the light-house so much that the stoves have to be lashed down. At night the ice breaking against the piers sounds like the cracking of fire.

Captain Lemuel Mitchell yesterday went to Thomas's Point from this place in a wagon, and there took the numbers of seven vessels dredging on that point contrary to law. To-day he is out probably searching up the delinquents.

The impact of the January 1877 ice emergency on Maryland's Chesapeake Bay maritime community was closely covered in Baltimore and Annapolis newspapers. This *Baltimore Sun* article included news of the oyster fleet, the deteriorating situation at Thomas Point and the activities of Captain Lemuel Mitchell of the Maryland Oyster Police. *From the* Baltimore Sun.

abandoning the damaged screwpile. Overhanging this decision was the fact that just four years earlier, keepers at the Love Point screwpile had abandoned their station in an ice floe. In later reviewing that situation, the Lighthouse Board determined that the men had left the Love Point station earlier than deemed appropriate. The keepers were dismissed for desertion. Eugene Burchenal had been the man assigned to replace the assistant keeper at Love Point. Burchenal and Miller knew the repercussions of an untimely abandonment, but the situation aboard their lighthouse continued to deteriorate.

The following day, Wednesday, January 17, the assault from the ice continued, and Burchenal made the call: it was too dangerous to stay aboard. Living conditions inside the house, after five full days of ice assault, had worn down the tired group. The cold returned and it was snowing. The lens was damaged, equipment and gear were strewn about and one of the screwpiles had broken. More of the supporting screwpiles looked vulnerable. The lighthouse leaned farther and farther at a wild angle.

Amid this chaos, Eugene Burchenal sat down and wrote a letter to Captain F.N. Baker, an official with the Lighthouse Board's Fifth District:

> *I regret to report that the ice came down on the house in very heavy fields at 9 o'clock A.M. on the morning of the 17th. Some of the ice over 2 feet thick pressing the house back and on the rebound snapped the cast iron cap on the south screwpile at the same time the lens was turned over and broken to pieces. The five hundred gal oil but was turned over and the oil spread all over the house. We had the lens lashed with back stays through the ventilator to the railing of the balcony it was no use. Nothing could stand that shaking up. I will try to stick to the house until further order. Will burn fixed white light in solas lamp until I get other orders. I recommend to the favor of the Light House board George A. Miller as first officer of this station in place of George E. Sullivan who has been absent one month today. I hope the Light House board will allow him pay as a laborer until he is regularly appointed he has stood by me on all this trouble brave and true he is very competent he knows what to do and when to do it and is willing to do it hope that his appointment may meet favorable consideration of the Light House Board.*

The group stuck it out through late afternoon of the next day, Thursday, January 18, before loading equipment into one of the station's tenders and voyaging more than a mile west through a moving field of drift ice to the shoreline at what remained of the Thomas Point peninsula.

The old tower, which had been abandoned just two years earlier in favor of the new screwpile on the shoal, still stood on the point, although high tides now swirled cold around its base. The keeper and his assistant climbed to the top of the broken-down stone tower on shore, and as evening approached, they lit a lamp at its top. Only then did Eugene Burchenal add a postscript to his letter:

> *January 18th captain left the light house at four o'clock p.m. this afternoon started the light at the old light station on shore to night will keep a light there until ordered to discontinue.*

On January 20, having received Burchenal's update, the Lighthouse Board published "Notice to Mariners No. 5 of 1877," headlined "Temporary Discontinuance of Thomas's Point Light." The notification informed mariners that the lighthouse "has been so injured by ice that it is necessary to temporarily discontinue the light."

A few days later, with the air still above freezing for much of the daylight hours, the ice field dissipated and then disappeared. On January 23, a work

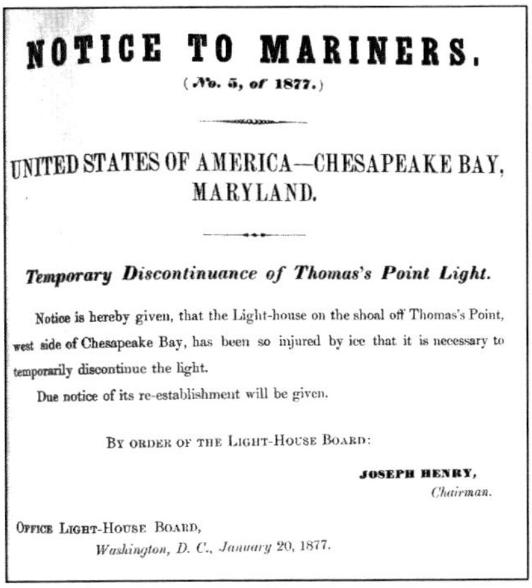

NOTICE TO MARINERS.

(No. 5, of 1877.)

UNITED STATES OF AMERICA—CHESAPEAKE BAY, MARYLAND.

Temporary Discontinuance of Thomas's Point Light.

Notice is hereby given, that the Light-house on the shoal off Thomas's Point, west side of Chesapeake Bay, has been so injured by ice that it is necessary to temporarily discontinue the light.

Due notice of its re-establishment will be given.

BY ORDER OF THE LIGHT-HOUSE BOARD:

JOSEPH HENRY,
Chairman.

OFFICE LIGHT-HOUSE BOARD,
Washington, D. C., January 20, 1877.

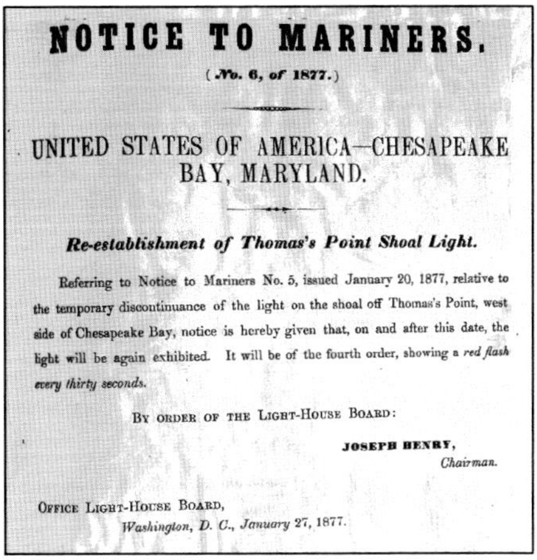

NOTICE TO MARINERS.

(No. 6, of 1877.)

UNITED STATES OF AMERICA—CHESAPEAKE BAY, MARYLAND.

Re-establishment of Thomas's Point Shoal Light.

Referring to Notice to Mariners No. 5, issued January 20, 1877, relative to the temporary discontinuance of the light on the shoal off Thomas's Point, west side of Chesapeake Bay, notice is hereby given that, on and after this date, the light will be again exhibited. It will be of the fourth order, showing a *red flash every thirty seconds.*

BY ORDER OF THE LIGHT-HOUSE BOARD:

JOSEPH HENRY,
Chairman.

OFFICE LIGHT-HOUSE BOARD,
Washington, D. C., January 27, 1877.

Left: In late January 1877, ice floes damaged the new screwpile structure at Thomas Point to such extent that its keepers were forced to extinguish the light and abandon the station. Upon receiving the news, the Lighthouse Board hurried to issue "Notice to Mariners Number 5 of 1877," which announced the discontinuance of the light. *U.S. National Archives and Records Administration.*

Right: Once week after Lighthouse Board's "Notice to Mariners Number 5 of 1877," which announced the discontinuance of the light at Thomas Point Shoal, having made the repairs to equipment and cleaned up the cottage, the Lighthouse Board published "Notice to Mariners Number 6 of 1877," which announced that "the light will again be exhibited" at the lighthouse on the shoal. *U.S. National Archives and Records Administration.*

crew traveled from Baltimore to Thomas Point on a steamer and inspected the chaos wrought by a ten-day ice siege. They walked across floors slippery with oil and inspected the damaged Fresnel lens. Beneath the cottage, they found some broken iron but determined that the structure was sound and in its proper spot.

The gear was put back in order, a replacement Fourth Order Fresnel was installed and the lighthouse was back in business. "Notice to Mariners No. 6 of 1877," titled "Re-establishment of Thomas's Point Shoal Light," was published on January 27, 1877.

One week after Burchenal and the Millers escaped the screwpile and relit the old tower, George Sullivan was "removed" from his position as first assistant keeper. Within the next two weeks, Charles Miller was promoted to first assistant, and George Miller, not yet twenty years old, was named second assistant keeper. Of special interest is the word *removed*. Although it sounds thoroughly negative, lighthouse historian Sandy Clunies noted that the word "does not imply incompetence or dereliction of duty—although it can do so." In his letter to the Lighthouse Board, Burchenal made it abundantly clear that Sullivan had been absent, unexpectedly, for an extended period of time.

Clunies added that "[k]eepers *were* removed for cause—for violence or fighting on duty, stealing, selling government issue fuel oil on the side, being inattentive to the light...ship captains would report dark lights and investigations were then conducted."

The problem of keepers abandoning their stations was of such concern that in February 1879, Silas W. Terry, a United States Coast Guard inspector, issued the following warning to keepers in his district:

> *As there appears to be a miss apprehension* [sic] *on the part of some Light Keepers as to their duty under circumstances when the Station is endangered by ice or other causes, they are reminded that this position of Light Keeper is one of danger, as well as trust, that they must remain by their light as long as the house stands; and if they are dismissed to do so, it is better to resign now, rather than be dismissed for desertion, when danger arises.*

Even after surviving and performing their duties admirably throughout the ice emergency, the risks faced by keepers such as Eugene Burchenal and others were not over. The life of a lighthouse keeper could be dangerous, even in warmer weather.

On Thursday, April 3, 1879, Eugene Burchenal and young George Miller were sailing from the lighthouse to Annapolis through a building storm when a gust of wind capsized their small vessel. It is known that Burchenal could not swim. The two men clung to the bottom of the overturned boat for nearly two hours before they were able to reach shore. The exhausted men were transported to Annapolis in a wagon.

Just two months later, Burchenal experienced another difficult sail to Annapolis. He was transferred between multiple boats as he moved from Thomas Point to Greenbury Point, where he secured a small boat for the final leg into Annapolis. However, in a building wind, the keeper became fearful that his small boat would be pulled out into the open water of the Bay. He then fell, or jumped, into the shallow water and safely made it to shore on foot. Both of the aforementioned incidents were noteworthy enough that they were reported in Annapolis newspapers.

The 1880 census shows Burchenal as single and living with an older couple as a boarder at 12 Cornhill Street, Annapolis. This pre–Revolutionary War row house is in the vicinity of the Annapolis City

Dock and still stands at this writing. That census listed his occupation as "Lighthouse Keeper."

Eugene Burchenal died, at age forty, in Annapolis on March 31, 1881. He is buried at St. Anne's Cemetery on College Creek in Annapolis, about six miles northwest of the lighthouse. The markings on his gravestone include the following declarative sentence:

All is well.

THE OYSTER WARS TURN DEADLY

In the fall of 1877, Captain Lemuel Mitchell entered his fifth season as a member of the Oyster Navy. Winter approached, with high oyster prices and rising tensions between law enforcement and watermen. In mid-December foul weather, an Oyster Navy vessel capsized and sank in the Chester River, to the northeast of Annapolis.

A few days before Christmas 1877, after a stretch of foul weather finally blew itself out, the oyster fleet returned to the Bay. During a break in the weather, Captain Patrick Kelly filled the hold of the Baltimore pungy *Two Brothers* with oysters illegally dredged on the Chester River and then turned to sail out of the river to the open Bay. As *Two Brothers* moved out of the Chester, Lemuel Mitchell and *Nannie Merryman* entered the river. Mitchell verbally ordered the pungy to halt, but Kelly claimed he did not hear the hail. Mitchell and crew shot across *Two Brothers*' bow and then into its rigging, but the pungy continued forward. Its crew later claimed that they had to lie down on the deck to keep from being shot and could not halt the vessel. Mitchell later reported that he and his crew had seen an arm and hand emerging from *Two Brothers*' cabin to hold its tiller and steer.

During the exchange, a ball shot from *Nannie Merryman* entered *Two Brothers*' cabin and hit thirty-five-year-old Baltimore oysterman William "Brocky Bill" Stewart in the left eye. The ball exited through his ear, tearing away part of the skull. Despite the gruesome wound, Stewart survived the shot, but he was in bad shape. The chase was halted, and *Two Brothers* surrendered. Kelly, Brocky Bill and the balance of *Two Brothers*' crew were removed to Chestertown, where Brocky Bill died in jail. With a well-known oysterman now dead on the Eastern Shore, the battle between the Oyster Navy and the Baltimore oyster industry entered a new phase.

Lemuel Mitchell was not the first Oyster Navy official to shoot at or kill a poacher, but the outcry from Baltimore over the Brocky Bill Stewart incident was swift and strong. In early January, the Maryland Board of State Fishing Force determined that Mitchell had not exercised proper discretion in the use of firearms. The board's censure was clear: "Whilst the board wishes to express its appreciation of the efficient service which Captain Mitchell has rendered during the past years, they feel constrained in the present instance to express their disapproval of his action and, therefore, are compelled to ask for his resignation."

The Baltimore political machine had won a round in the ongoing battle. Mitchell wrote out his resignation. However, Lemuel Mitchell knew that he had unfinished business and postdated his resignation to an effective date of May 1878—the end of his current commission and four months in the future. Although the Baltimore contingent certainly howled, the unique arrangement suited the board, and Mitchell was almost immediately back aboard the *Merryman*.

Just four weeks after the Chester River incident, Mitchell and the *Nannie Merryman* were at Thomas Point on January 16, 1878. In the early morning light, Mitchell spotted a Baltimore pungy illegally dredging within one and a half miles of the Thomas Point shoreline. The pungy turned out to be *Maid of Erin*, led by Captain Andrew Conroy and manned by four other Baltimore oystermen. Conroy, in his early forties, was the father of four children, a veteran oysterman and apparently a member of a well-known family of Baltimore fishermen and watermen.

After sighting the approaching *Nannie*, Conroy and *Maid of Erin* bolted. Mitchell gave chase and began firing at the pungy around 8:00 a.m., within sight of the Thomas Point Shoal Lighthouse. Unlike the crew of *Two Brothers*, which claimed that the shots from *Nannie* came in a rush, the crew of *Maid of Erin* later claimed that the shots fired at it in a calm and deliberate manner. As Captain Conroy manned the fleeing pungy's tiller, shots passed close by on either side of him before one struck him in the right side. The *Maid of Erin* crew later claimed that the shot had been aimed intentionally.

The chase was over. Conroy was paralyzed below the waist and in great pain. Lemuel Mitchell accompanied the Baltimore man to Annapolis, where the poacher was carried to jail. Captain Conroy's wound was deemed quite serious; a probe for the ball yielded no results. A priest was called

Unloading oyster boats and moving the harvest into a shucking facility at Baltimore, circa 1905. *Library of Congress.*

from nearby St. Mary's Catholic Church, and last rites were administered. The *Baltimore Sun* provided its readers with a detailed account of the scene: "The anointing for death presented a solemn scene in the prison-room....The agonizing groans of the unfortunate man mingled with the solemn prayer of the priest." Conroy's brothers came down from Baltimore and took the gravely wounded captain home, where a fury brewed.

In the immediate wake of the second shooting, Lemuel Mitchell again resigned but once again listed May 1 as his date of resignation. At this point, that date was more than three months in the future, on the backside of the current oyster season. The crowd at Baltimore had earlier found the death

FRANK LESLIE'S ILLUSTRATED NEWSPAPER

No. 1,686.—VOL. LXV.] NEW YORK—FOR THE WEEK ENDING JANUARY 7, 1888. [PRICE, 10 CENTS.

MARYLAND.—THE OYSTER WAR—A STATE POLICE STEAMER OVERHAULING A PIRATE BOAT ON CHESAPEAKE BAY, OFF SWAN'S POINT.

FROM A SKETCH BY FRANK ADAMS.—SEE PAGE 349.

The cover of the January 7, 1888 edition of *Frank Leslie's Illustrated Newspaper* portrays a pair of men on a police boat arresting two men who are illegally oystering, a scene that might have been modeled on Lemuel Mitchell's activity on Thomas Point Shoal. *Library of Congress.*

of unmarried Brocky Bill Stewart troubling, but the shooting of Conroy, a popular father of four from a well-known family, worked the Baltimore waterfront into a froth. As Conroy lay near death in his home at Fells Point, a group of angry oystermen gathered and denounced the shooting. They appointed a committee to travel to Annapolis and demand the immediate dismissal of Mitchell. Meanwhile, at Annapolis, the full Baltimore city delegation to the Maryland legislature, headed by the three senators, met with Maryland's governor to protest against Captain Mitchell. "A great deal of indignation has been expressed in the Legislature on account of the violent use of firearms by the oyster police force and especially by Captain Mitchell," an Annapolis newspaper reported.

The members of the Baltimore delegation demanded Mitchell's immediate removal and insisted that he should be charged as a civilian in the Conroy shooting. A spokesman for the delegation told the governor that the oyster police vessels and crews are supplied with firearms *only* for defense and in the case of resistance, but they were now being used recklessly to shoot at people in quiet pursuit of their business. The Oyster Navy, the delegation asserted, and especially Lemuel Mitchell, had taken their powers too far.

Maryland's governor assured the Baltimore men that he was aware of the situation and of Mitchell. Even as this conversation took place, the Board of State Fishing Force convened a special session to discuss the situation. Aware of the anger and political might of the Baltimore contingent, the board demanded Mitchell's instant removal. A new commander was immediately assigned to the *Nannie Merryman*, and Mitchell's state pay was stopped. The shooting was mentioned in multiple newspapers, including the *New York Herald*, which noted, "This is the second man shot by Mitchell in four months." It had actually only been four *weeks* between Mitchell's shooting of Brocky Bill and his shooting of Andrew Conroy.

By mid-February, Andrew Conroy had died of his wounds. His case had become something of a cause célèbre among the Baltimore waterfront community—a stunning case, many believed, of law enforcement overreach. The *Baltimore Sun* now called Conroy's death "a murder" and reported that his wife and children were living "in destitute condition." Conroy's funeral took place at the family home, on Pleasant Alley in the Fells Point section of Baltimore. The *Sun* reported, "The funeral was attended by a large number of vessel captains and oystermen." The *Sun*'s report did, however, note that Conroy had been shot "while illegally dredging off Thomas's Point," a fact that perhaps gave Captain Mitchell some solace. Meanwhile, back at Annapolis, where Lemuel Mitchell was generally viewed as an efficient and popular law enforcement officer, a growing number of people wanted to see the captain finish out his term.

The legal repercussions soon faded away, and somehow, Lemuel Mitchell returned to the water, with his resignation again set for May 1. In April, on what must have been one of his final patrols as a state employee, Mitchell encountered a pair of Baltimore pungies, the *Flora Thomas* and the *Luther T. Harding*. Both were illegally dredging, and predictably, a confrontation ensued. Shots were exchanged in both directions. When the smoke cleared, Thomas W. Moore, master of the *Flora Thomas*, was charged and found guilty of assaulting Captain Mitchell. The master of the *Luther T. Harding* was found guilty of illegal dredging. His name was Michael Conroy.

On May 1, 1878, Lemuel Mitchell's commission expired, and after five wild years, he relinquished command of the *Nannie Merryman*. The *Merryman* continued to serve as part of Maryland's state fleet into the twentieth century. Mitchell, it appears, returned to life as an Annapolis waterman.

Multiple newspaper reports have been located that illustrate Mitchell's activity on the water outside of his Oyster Navy duties. When not engaged in his official duties, Lemuel Mitchell raised his family in Annapolis and was part of the local community. On July 4, 1874, the citizens of Annapolis celebrated the holiday with a series of sailboat races in the Severn River and on the Chesapeake Bay. A midday contest was a match race between a pair of sloops that raced from the Annapolis Harbor out to the Thomas Point buoy and back, a total of sixteen miles. Between eighteen and twenty men sailed aboard each sloop in a lively breeze, and a large crowd awaited at the finish line off the Annapolis docks. The afternoon contest was a ten-mile race from the harbor out to Tolly Point and back. It featured three sloops, including the *Nannie Merryman*, led by Captain Lemuel Mitchell. *Merryman* was first to finish.

In mid-July 1876, while off-season from his Oyster Navy duties, Captain Mitchell and several other fishermen caught more than 1,400 white perch and sold them on the docks at Annapolis.

In mid-August 1878, shortly after his Oyster Navy commission expired, Lem Mitchell was hauling fishing nets at the mouth of the Severn River near what is now Lake Ogleton, at Tolly Point when he captured an eight-foot-long shark weighing about three hundred pounds. Mitchell secured the shark to the side of his boat and towed it to the wharf at Annapolis, where he exhibited it. A newspaper account remarked, "It has a savage appearance about the head and face." Mitchell presumably charged a fee to view the

FRANK LESLIE'S ILLUSTRATED NEWSPAPER

NEW YORK, OCTOBER 23, 1880.

Joseph Becker's illustration, captioned "'In the Mornin' by de Bright Light,' Negro Oystermen of Annapolis on their way to the Fishing-Ground in Chesapeake Bay," graced the cover of *Frank Leslie's Illustrated Newspaper* on October 22, 1880. *Library of Congress.*

shark, as the paper went on to report, "From the number of curiosity seekers we presume it will be a rather profitable fish for the captain."

Mitchell remained close to the oyster trade and was a champion of those involved in the legal oyster business. In 1887, he led a drive for a city-purchased tugboat to help Annapolis oystermen efficiently get to and from approved oyster grounds. In 1891, he was listed as a member of the police force at the thriving Bay Ridge resort, located just southeast of Annapolis.

There are multiple reports of the Anne Arundel county sheriff engaging Lemuel Mitchell to serve arrest warrants on poachers well into the 1880s. In the winter of 1888, poachers were again taking advantage of icy conditions to illegally dredge at Thomas Point Shoal. "For several days it has been reported that the dredgers have been playing havoc with Thomas' Point," the *Evening Capital* newspaper reported. Onlookers from shore had counted at least a dozen boats illegally dredging. The Anne Arundel county sheriff and "a posse" boarded a tugboat in an operation to engage the poachers, but the tug was soon locked in by the ice at the point. The State of Maryland–owned steamship *Governor McLane* arrived in Annapolis to join the activity and, presumably, rescue the tugboat and challenge the poachers. When the *Governor McLane* crew refused to go out in the dangerous conditions, a crew of Annapolis men, led by fifty-four-year-old Lemuel Mitchell, took command of the steamship and set out for Thomas Point. Despite their best efforts, they were unable to capture any poachers.

After he left the Oyster Navy, Lemuel and Rachel Mitchell remained in the Eastport section of Annapolis. They celebrated their fiftieth anniversary on January 1, 1910. The 1910 Annapolis City Directory listed Lemuel Mitchell's occupation as "Waterman."

Lemuel Mitchell died at his home in Eastport on July 24, 1911. His death was reported in a small item on the front page of the *Evening Capital* newspaper. The report mentioned his service aboard the *Nannie Merryman* and referred to him as "an old and respected citizen."

LIVING ABOARD

1800s

Lighthouses are endlessly suggestive signifiers of both human isolation and our ultimate connectedness to each other.
—often attributed to Virginia Woolf, although the source is apocryphal

Lighthouses captured the American imagination and helped fuel its economy. The American lighthouse infrastructure and system of navigational aids, once woefully lagging behind those in Europe, had recovered from the Civil War and developed into a cohesive network featuring modern technology and managed to high standards by the United States Lighthouse Board.

Beginning in May 1876, just six months after the commissioning of the Thomas Point screwpile, the United States Lighthouse Board participated in the Centennial International Exposition at Philadelphia, a sprawling world's fair timed to coincide with the 100th anniversary of the signing of the Declaration of Independence. The showcasing of lighthouse equipment and technology at international fairs had become something of a tradition. The twelve-foot-tall First Order Cape Hatteras Fresnel lens was displayed at the 1853 world's fair at New York City, and in 1867, both the French and the British lighthouse establishments built and displayed lighthouse towers at the world's fair at Paris.

The 1876 fair was held in the northwest suburbs of Philadelphia in a park on the edge of the Schuylkill River. Event organizers assigned the Lighthouse Board a position in the interior of the park, at the edge of a marshy lake, about one thousand yards inland from the river. This location—close to the main entrance and the New York, California and British government buildings—was certain to attract a steady flow of visitors. In anticipation, the Lighthouse Board pulled out all the stops. Examples of the service's latest buoys were set up in the open air. Nearby, Fresnel lenses, station models, equipment and signaling devices were displayed inside a building that had been erected especially for the event. A recap of the exposition referenced the exhibit, noting, "The eye was at once attracted in passing by the beautiful display of lanterns....The general shape of these lanterns is much like an exaggerated pineapple."

The most modern fogbells and sirens were displayed and frequently sounded. A steam-powered foghorn announced the daily opening and closing of the exhibition grounds. "When it sounded," one attendee noted, "there was no mistaking the hour." At the center of the exhibit, serving as a can't-miss-it landmark for fairgoers, stood a fully equipped American lighthouse, open and available for touring. The cast-iron caisson lighthouse superstructure had been built for the Ship John Shoal in the nearby Delaware Bay and then diverted to inland Philadelphia for this unique duty. Throughout the event, uniformed lighthouse keepers tended the light, ensuring that it was properly illuminated every night to the standards of the Lighthouse Board.

The public adored the exposition, and nearly 10 million visitors flowed through the gates over the six-month run. Lighthouse Board officials were thrilled with the reception and included news of the exhibit in its 1876 report to Congress:

> *The station was visited by a multitude of people, whom its unique devices greatly interested. Among them were many persons of distinction from foreign nations interested in nautical affairs, including several officers of life-saving institutions in other countries, who examined minutely into all details of our entire system, which some of them volunteered to say was unequalled by any system in the world. Interested dignitaries and officers were provided with plans and specifications for lighthouse stations and associated gear and apparatus.*

The new American Lighthouse Establishment had arrived and was receiving global recognition.

Ironically, the shoal at Ship John, Delaware Bay, was originally slated to receive a screwpile lighthouse, but the board's negative experience with

Lighthouses and the expansion of the lighthouse network captured the American imagination, from symbolic, technological and practical perspectives. A new cast-iron caisson lighthouse superstructure built for the Ship John Shoal in Delaware Bay was sent inland to Philadelphia for display at the 1876 International Exhibition, celebrating the centennial of the founding of the United States. *Library of Congress.*

screwpiles in the ice led it to change the plans to a sturdier caisson. Congress approved the change. Following the exhibition, the caisson superstructure displayed at the Centennial Exposition was moved to Ship John Shoal, where it remains in place.

DURING THE RAPID ECONOMIC expansion after the Civil War, the Port of Baltimore and the Chesapeake Bay lighthouse network became even more critical components in the nation's commerce. Inbound cargos from Europe and South America arrived at Baltimore on regular schedules, as did a flood of immigrants. In 1882 alone, more than forty-two thousand immigrants entered at Baltimore.

Baltimore's century-long expansion had relegated the port of Annapolis to a much smaller role. While the U.S. Naval Academy had been established on the Annapolis waterfront in 1845 and provided the city with a jolt of population and waterborne activity, by the 1870s there were few, if any, cargos loaded and unloaded on the Annapolis wharves, aside from oysters and fish. In early 1877, an editorial in the Annapolis-based *Maryland Republican* declared, "Before the genius of Baltimore, the star of Annapolis paled into an insignificant commercial luminary and her harbor became merely the refuge of a few small coasters instead of the grand depot of trade she was destined by nature to become."

While nearby Annapolis remained somewhat languid, the new lighthouse at nearby Thomas Point, its base structure having survived the ice emergency and now reinforced to protect against future ice events, unwaveringly served its important role. The Lighthouse Board's 1878 "Light List" described the Thomas Point Shoal Lighthouse in a straightforward manner: "A hexagonal screw-pile light-house. Foundation painted brown; superstructure, white; roof, brown; lantern, red. The light-house stands on 9 screw-piles, in 8 feet of water."

Although natural beauty surrounded the lighthouse and the position offered the opportunity for sober self-reflection, life aboard the station could be a tedious run of cleaning, painting, recording log book entries and, most importantly, refilling the fuel to keep the light in order. Although keeper wives and families were permitted to live aboard in the early years—Assistant Keeper Miller's wife and teenage son were aboard during the ice emergency of 1877—Thomas Point was a lonely station, despite its proximity to Annapolis. Two to four keepers were typically assigned, and they worked in split shifts, with a keeper or two manning the lighthouse while another keeper or two were ashore. The lighthouse was never left unattended (although a member of a keeper's family "or other responsible person" could man the station, if necessary).

BY THE FALL OF 1876, the Lighthouse Board had created fifty portable libraries, each holding about forty books and created for keepers assigned to the more isolated stations. A library remained at a station for about six months and then was rotated away as a fresh collection arrived. Some of the books had been donated by private citizens, while others were purchased by the Lighthouse Board. The board explained in its annual report to Congress, "By this means the keepers will be constantly supplied with fresh and interesting reading matter and be made contented with the lonely life and routing duties of these distant and often inaccessible stations." A replica of one of these traveling libraries is currently on the station at Thomas Point.

IN JULY 1881, THE Lighthouse Board published its "Instructions to Light-Keepers," which provides a detailed look at the roles and responsibilities of the men serving aboard at Thomas Point Shoal. Given the somewhat militaristic nature of the Lighthouse Board, the relatively high profile of the new lighthouse and its proximity to Annapolis, Baltimore and Washington, it is likely that the Thomas Point keepers adhered closely to these instructions. Keepers and assistant keepers were given each a copy of the instructions, and they were, according to a notice at the front of the publication, "required to read them carefully and attentively."

The Lighthouse Board had, by this point, seen it all, resulting in published instructions often written in a quite specific manner. Day-to-day duties and responsibilities are explicitly spelled out:

> *All keepers must acquaint themselves with the workings of the apparatus in their charge. Upon any doubtful point, questions must be asked. When the station is visited by an officer or employee of the Light-House Establishment, especially while the machinist or lampist is there, the keepers must take pains to acquire knowledge of every detail regarding the mechanism of the apparatus.*
>
> *…The keeper is responsible for the careful management and expenditure of stores and supplies. He must practice the strictest economy compatible with maintaining at all times the best possible light.*

Occasional visitors were expected, and the keeper was required to be "courteous and polite" to them and "show them everything of interest about the station as such times as it will not interfere with lighthouse duties." No visitors were permitted to enter the lamp room without a keeper present. Keepers were not permitted to charge for admission to the lighthouse: "The utmost neatness of buildings and premises is demanded…untidiness will be strongly reprimanded and its continuance will subject a keeper to dismissal."

Boats were provided to the keepers but only for lighthouse purposes. "The boats must not be used for freighting, wrecking, fishing with seines, ferrying, or for carrying goods or passengers for hire."

Detailed instructions were specified for painting, cleaning, polishing and washing. All important, above all else, was the light. The lamp was lit promptly at sunset and kept burning at full intensity until sunrise. After the light was extinguished, the keeper had to hang curtains in the lamp room windows and begin preparations for its relighting, including a daily cleaning. Keepers completed these lamp-related chores while wearing linen aprons, provided and required to keep the treasured lens from contacting everyday clothing. Status reports were filed monthly. Expense reports were due quarterly.

The station's logbook recorded daily weather information, delivery of provisions and "any item of interest in the area." The logbook "must be kept in ink, with neatness and must always be kept up to date."

THE 1881 ANNUAL FOOD ration, per man, included, among other things, forty-five pounds each of pork and beef, sixty-five pounds of ship biscuits, six and a half pounds of raisins, six pounds of coffee, two and a half bushels of potatoes, a bushel of onions and six pounds of pickles. Rainwater for drinking, bathing and cleaning was collected off the roof and funneled into four cisterns.

Even with a lengthy list of specific official duties, there was a fair amount of free time on the lighthouse. It is known that nineteenth-century lighthouse keepers fished, played cards and read books at the station. The consumption of alcohol was prohibited. Most of the early keepers seem to have been from the Baltimore and Annapolis area, so when not on station at Thomas Point, they returned ashore to stay with their families and friends.

At the turn of the twentieth century, the keepers of Thomas Point continued to work for the Lighthouse Board's Fifth District, which covered the Mid-Atlantic states, and the majority of the district's keepers were from the Mid-Atlantic. Because keepers were rotated through the district, it became possible for North Carolina–based keepers to be assigned stints at Thomas Point and other Maryland stations.

A PROPERLY MAINTAINED AND tended lighthouse is most successful if is *not* featured in news reports. A lack of mishaps and an absence of drama at and near a station indicate success. The screwpile on the Thomas Point

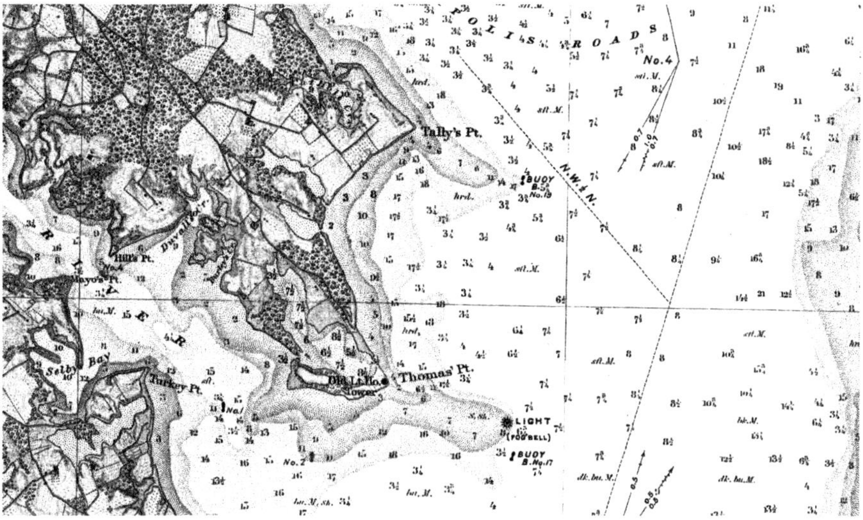

Detail of an 1884 nautical chart showing the new lighthouse and fog bell on the end of the shoal, with buoy no. 17 nearby and the old lighthouse tower on the rapidly eroding tip of Thomas Point. *National Archives and Records Administration.*

Major Jared A. Smith took this photograph of the not-yet-ten-year-old Thomas Point Shoal Lighthouse at 6:00 a.m. on August 18, 1885. The view is northwest. The ice breaker has been installed on the northern side of the screwpile, but no riprap is in place. *National Archives and Records Administration.*

Shoal, in large part, operated efficiently and stayed out of the press, but it was occasionally in the news for mundane reasons. In December 1893, the *Baltimore Sun* reported that a wild duck had flown against a large pane of glass at the lantern room of the Thomas Point lighthouse "with such force as to smash the glass though it was a quarter of an inch thick and five feet square." The Fresnel lens was damaged in the incident. While awaiting repairs, the keepers plugged the hole with a small sail. The bird, the *Sun* reported, "dropped dead on the inside, after finishing its destructive work. It was probably a straggler that had been attracted by the bright light at the lighthouse as no other ducks could be seen by the keepers."

In 1899, a "new model" Fourth Order Fresnel lens was installed at Thomas Point. A Fourth Order Fresnel stands nearly three feet tall and weighs several hundred pounds. By 1900, 350 of them were in place in U.S. lighthouses, including the one atop the Thomas Point screwpile. It stayed in place at the station for eighty-seven years.

The Fresnel lenses represented a real investment by the federal government. In 1900, a French-made First Order Fresnel lens cost the Lighthouse Board $12,500 (about $382,000 in 2020 dollars). At the same time, a smaller Fourth Order lens was a relative bargain, costing the Lighthouse Board $1,250 (about $38,000 in 2020 dollars).

The Lighthouse Board was moved from the Treasury Department into the new formed United States Department of Commerce in 1903. The existing Fifth District retained its name and its headquarters at Baltimore. The rotation of keepers throughout the district continued.

A KEEPER MYSTERIOUSLY DISAPPEARS

It gives you time to think about life, yourself,
and the purpose for being here on earth.
—John White, Thomas Point Shoal Lighthouse keeper, 1974

On Friday, July 3, 1903, the assistant keeper of the Thomas Point Shoal Lighthouse, Henry Addicks, made a scheduled trip into Annapolis aboard one of the station's tenders. The trip was routine. Reports were filed, groceries procured and mail received. Back in 1883, the staff manning Thomas Point station had been reduced from three to two when the second assistant keeper position was abolished. As a result, Addicks traveled to Annapolis alone, leaving Head Keeper Daniel White alone aboard the station. The two men had served together at Thomas Point for more than a year, and by midsummer of 1903, Henry Addicks had become very unhappy with life aboard the lighthouse. While no evidence exists of friction between Addicks and White, Addicks is said to have declared during his visit to Annapolis that he was desperate for a change. He was later described as "lonely" and "naturally melancholy."

Henry Addicks had immigrated to the Baltimore waterfront from Germany. He had arrived at Thomas Point in 1901 after a stint as the assistant keeper at the remote Holland Island Bar screwpile in southern Maryland. However, little is known of Addicks's life before his role on the Chesapeake Bay lighthouses. A person by the name of Henry Addicks is listed in the 1890 Baltimore City Directory as living in the Fells Point section

Thomas Point Shoal Lighthouse at sunset, September 2018. *Photo by the author.*

of the city and working as a "Laborer." A seaman named Henry Addicks was part of a dramatic rescue operation on the North Carolina Outer Banks during a hurricane in August 1899. It is unknown if either of these men later served two years at Thomas Point, but given the geography and the unique name, it is likely.

While stationed at Thomas Point, Addicks kept a room and a bank account in Baltimore, and he regularly corresponded with his relatives who remained in Germany, sending money back to them as frequently as possible. He also told his German relatives about his dissatisfaction in America and appears to have inquired about the current situation in Germany and the possibility of returning. Around the time of his early July visit to Annapolis, perhaps on that exact visit to Annapolis, Addicks received a letter from his brother Frederick, who had stayed behind in Germany. In this letter, Frederick advised Henry that a steady position on an American lighthouse was preferable to returning home, where wages were low and the prospects dim. The news only served to deepen Addicks's despondency.

Shortly after Henry Addicks's trip into Annapolis, Head Keeper Daniel White traveled into town for a scheduled break, leaving Addicks alone on the station. On Friday morning, July 10, around 11:00 a.m., White, still ashore, noticed that the light was still burning at the lighthouse. He studied the lighthouse with a pair of field glasses and attempted to signal the station. Growing more concerned about the situation, White and his twelve-year-old niece rowed out to the lighthouse. Aside from the light burning in the midmorning daylight, they found all in order aboard the station. However, there was no sign of Henry Addicks. His clothes and effects were in place, as were the station's two tenders, both hung in their davits with canvas covers in place.

Alarmed, the head keeper and his niece rowed to intercept the nearby steamer *Emma Giles*. The *Emma Giles* transported the girl to Annapolis, where she made a report of the situation. White later reported that Addicks had been despondent for some time and on several occasions had threatened suicide.

Word soon made its way to Baltimore, and Commander John Hawley, inspector of the Lighthouse Board's Fifth District, traveled to Thomas Point aboard the 164-foot lighthouse tender *Maple*. After investigating the situation, discovering the letters from Germany and receipts for the remittances back to Germany, Hawley declared that he believed Addicks had committed suicide by drowning and added that the missing man had made frequent remarks "that death was preferable to living."

The mysterious disappearance and the gruesome theory made headlines in Maryland. The *Baltimore Sun* led with Hawley's theory: "Thinks Keeper Committed Suicide." The *Cumberland (MD) Evening Times* chose the pulpier headline "Loneliness Drove Him Mad." The *Evening Capital* noted, "If the man jumped overboard his death would have been instantaneous as the water about the lighthouse abounds in rocks."

A few days later, Albert Groth, a longtime friend and roommate of Addicks's, traveled to the lighthouse, searching for clues and information. Groth looked through Addicks's effects and informed the lighthouse service that he would notify the relatives in Germany. He added that, in his opinion, the death was an accident, not a suicide. Henry Addicks, Groth attested, was generally a happy man and was satisfied with his position at the lighthouse. In the days after Addicks's disappearance, men dragged the shoal and the area around the lighthouse with oystering gear, searching for a body or a clue.

More than a century later, it is accepted as fact that while alone on the Thomas Point screwpile, Assistant Keeper Henry Addicks stripped to his underwear and then disappeared. His final moments were likely on the rocks or the railing of the lighthouse, and it remains unknown if he spent them intent on suicide or a simple cooling-off swim on a warm midsummer day. His body was never found.

Just eighteen months later, in late February 1905, Keeper White's successor, John Suit, had his own trouble with a Thomas Point assistant keeper. On February 26, Keeper Suit wrote to the inspector in Baltimore, "I am sorry to report that the assistant, Mr. Peter S. Earle, is losing his mind and I cannot trust him with the light he has worried me with his actions and talk very much. I think his case should be looked after I went ashore to the island and got Mr. George Tyler to come out and take him off the station."

Peter Earle had been at Thomas Point for less than four months, but the winter and the isolation were taking a toll. After a break ashore, the assistant keeper was returned to the station, but by early March, he went missing, having traveled to Annapolis by boat and not returned. Earle was relieved of his duties. It must have been a wearing winter because by March, Keeper

Thomas Point Shoal Lighthouse at sunrise, September 2019. *Photo by the author.*

Suit himself was asking for a transfer back to the Annapolis Buoy Depot, where he had previously been stationed. He ended up staying at Thomas Point for three more years.

During the following summer, a large sailing canoe capsized in the vicinity of the lighthouse. Captain Samuel Bullen was sailing home to the South River from a shopping trip to Annapolis, and his boat was loaded with provisions and dry goods. Keeper John Suit and his new assistant, Henry Wingate, launched a boat in a strong southeasterly wind and rescued Bullen. The keepers towed his boat ashore, where it was righted. Unfortunately, all the provisions and dry goods were lost. Suit and Wingate's efforts were commended in Baltimore and Washington.

The Lighthouse Board wrote a letter to Suit commending him for his act of bravery. The letter was signed by navy officer Uriel Sebree, a member of the Lighthouse Board. Two summers later, Sebree would advocate in Washington on Keeper Suit's behalf.

TONGERS TRESPASS AT THE LIGHT

In his extended term as keeper of the Thomas Point Shoal Lighthouse, and as an assistant keeper before that, John Suit had endured severe weather conditions and bizarre behavior from assistants. He had rescued distressed mariners from the water and had diligently kept the light, but by late summer 1907, he had reached his limit with the local watermen. While the high drama of the 1870s was decades in the past, oysters remained valuable, and they could still be found on the shoal, albeit in decreasing numbers. In early September 1907, the trouble on the shoal was not initiated by the rowdy crews of larger Baltimore oyster schooners, but rather by the local men aboard small boats. Searching for new bottom and more oysters, the men who worked the shoal—tongers in crews of one, two or three—pushed ever closer to the lighthouse itself.

Keeper Suit watched this activity from aboard the station. The actual property of the lighthouse reservation, including the bottom of the Chesapeake, is circular and covers five full acres, extending more than 263 feet outward, in all directions, from the center of the screwpile. The tongers began working the bottom inside of the lighthouse property.

When Suit informed the oystermen that they were taking oysters inside of the lighthouse property lines—likely in uniform and shouting from the edge of the main-level gallery—he was answered with jeers. The frustrated keeper recorded identifying details of each encroaching boat and forwarded the list, along with his report, to Baltimore. Seventeen different boat names are on the list. They hailed from Eastport, Annapolis

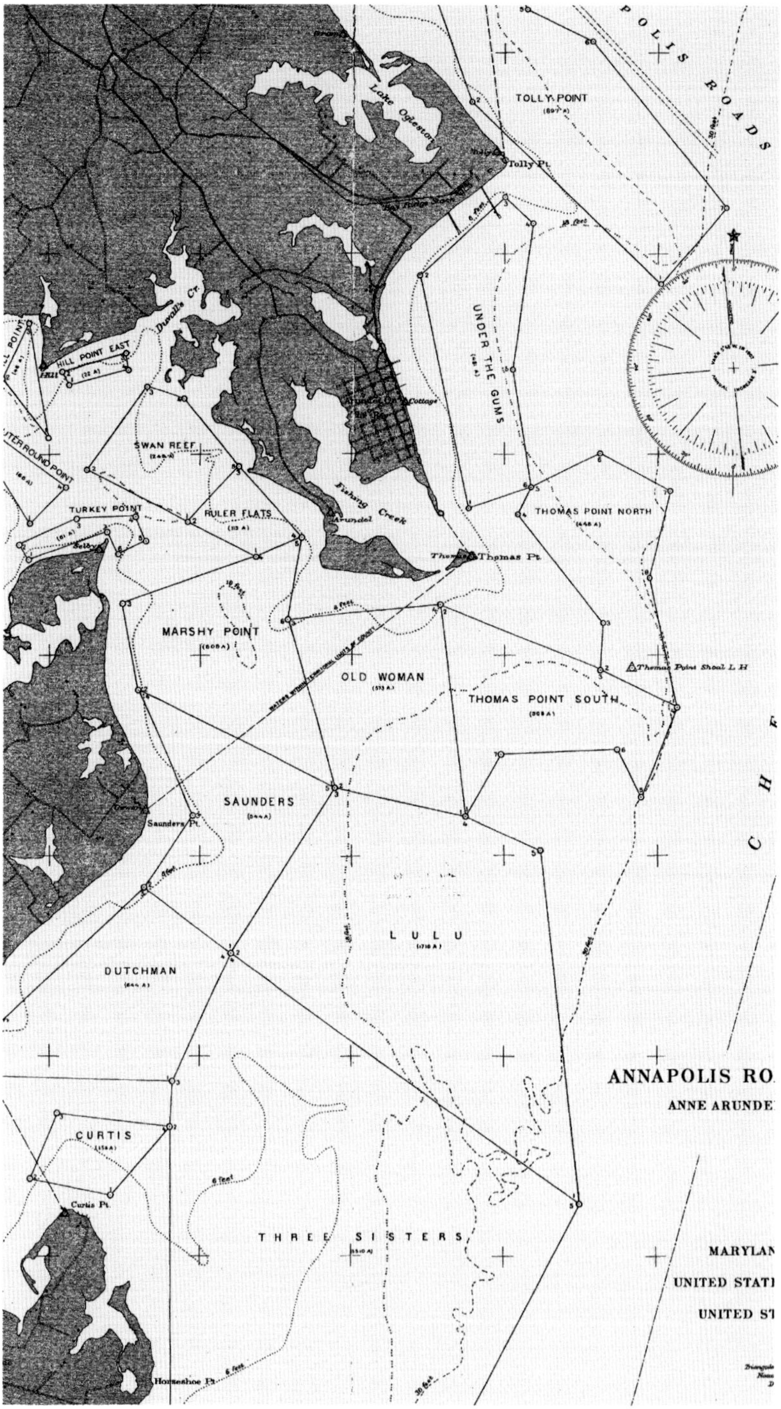
TOLLY POINT
Tolly Pt.
Lake Ogleston
UNDER THE GUMS
HILL POINT EAST
SWAN REEF
TURKEY POINT
RULER FLATS
Fishing Creek
Thomas Pt.
THOMAS POINT NORTH
MARSHY POINT
OLD WOMAN
THOMAS POINT SOUTH
Thomas Point Shoal L.H.
SAUNDERS
Saunders Pt.
LULU
DUTCHMAN
CURTIS
Curtis Pt.
THREE SISTERS
Horseshoe Pt.
ANNAPOLIS RO
ANNE ARUNDE
MARYLAN
UNITED STAT
UNITED ST

Above: Oyster tongers "Working the beds off Annapolis," as drawn by M.J. Burns and published in *Harper's Weekly* on January 11, 1890. This scene would have been familiar to the keepers of the Thomas Point Shoal Lighthouse. *Library of Congress.*

Opposite: Detail of a 1906 chart illustrating the oyster bars in the Chesapeake Bay in the vicinity of Thomas Point. The chart also shows the site of the Thomas Point tower as a complete island. *National Archives and Records Administration.*

and the nearby West River. The encroaching watercraft, when described by Suit, are listed as "Canoe," "Bateau" and "deadrise boat." Eleven men are listed by their name. Twenty more are unnamed and listed as "white man," "colored men" and "boy."

On September 9, officials in Baltimore forwarded the report and the list to the Lighthouse Board in Washington, D.C., and asked if there was legal means to prevent these men from taking oysters inside of the lighthouse property lines.

The reply came directly from Oscar Straus, President Theodore Roosevelt's secretary of commerce and labor, the man at the head of the federal department within which the Lighthouse Board operated. Straus called the complaint "very trivial" and noted that unless the taking of oysters within the lighthouse reservation "in some way interferes with the efficiency of the light-house service or damages the property of the government...the department is not inclined to take any notice of the matter."

Straus's reply was, apparently, deemed unsatisfactory by district officials in Baltimore and by members of the Lighthouse Board itself. Four days after Secretary Straus's memorandum, Rear Admiral Uriel Sebree, a member of the Lighthouse Board, replied to Straus in writing. Sebree, an 1867 Naval Academy graduate, had been part of two Artic expeditions and served as commander in chief of the Pacific Fleet. Now, in his late career role on the Lighthouse Board, he leveraged his considerable authority and gravitas to directly respond to the situation at Thomas Point, perhaps recalling Keeper Suit from the letter of commendation he had written just two years earlier when Suit rescued the capsized mariner.

Sebree asked that Straus reconsider the matter and fleshed out the specifics of the reservation and the situation. He added, "To permit trespassers on this light-house reservation would be in contravention to the long-established policy of the board."

Two days later, Secretary Straus, politely reproached by his own lighthouse board and reminded of its political power, responded, "In view of the facts of the case, and in accordance with your recommendation, the Board is hereby authorized to instruct the Inspector of the Fifth Light-House District to notify the parties referred to in his letter...that in trespassing on the Thomas Point Reservation they are violating the laws and regulations of the Light-House Establishment; and to report future cases of trespass on this reservation, together with the names of the parties and dates thereof, for the action of the board and the Department."

Keeper John Suit could now address trespassers with the full weight of the Lighthouse Board and the Department of Commerce behind him, although no record of any further conflicts or action has been located.

IN 1910, THE LIGHTHOUSE Board was disbanded, as Congress was moving toward to a more civilian-led Lighthouse Service under the Department of Commerce. It was believed that the long-term service of civilian employees would provide needed continuity in the management of America's lighthouse network. The existing Fifth District retained its name and its headquarters at Baltimore.

Despite the multiple projects designed to build up the rubble at the station's base, including a large 1886–87 project to place 1,600 cubic yards

Detail of riprap and ice breaker piling on the north side of the Thomas Point Shoal Lighthouse structure, as seen on March 20, 1918. *National Archives and Records Administration.*

of riprap beneath the cottage, ice continued to damage the lighthouse at Thomas Point. In 1919, the Lighthouse Service undertook an $1,800 project to "Restore light station to original strength." The recommendation noted, "The braces on this structure are badly deteriorated due to ice action at the lower ends. The ice piling up around the structure last winter broke two of them and the structure is greatly weakened due to the condition of the others. The ladders were demolished last winter by the ice."

THE POINT BREAKS UP AND IS SOLD OFF

At the time the two stone lighthouse towers were built on it, the Thomas Point peninsula was an arrow-shaped stretch of sandy land enclosing a broad lake, unnamed on many early charts but called Fishing Creek at least as early as 1878. There is a report that the first breakthrough from the Bay into Fishing Creek at Thomas Point came as early as 1856. It is likely that the Bay broke through regularly at high tides and, in storms, even before that. An 1855 U.S. Geological Survey chart shows the land at the tip of the point nearly severed from the mainland.

As the twentieth century approached, land erosion at the point accelerated, as two or more breaks became semipermanent, making overland access to the old tower challenging if not impossible. By 1890, the land around the old tower had been cut off, permanently it seems, forming an island around the tower.

This easily accessed but remote island became a magnet for waterfowlers, especially duck hunters, who clamored for the right to erect duck blinds on the government property and in adjacent waters. By 1891, the nearby community of Arundel-on-the-Bay had been chartered, and building lots were being marketed and sold. Summer residents enjoyed accessing the sandy island for picnics and excursions; the ruins of the second tower added to the adventuresome ambiance. The federal government received a flurry of inquiries from developers, duck hunters and, sometimes, their attorneys, all of whom inquired as to its plans for the property and jockeyed for the right to purchase the eroding but coveted bit of land.

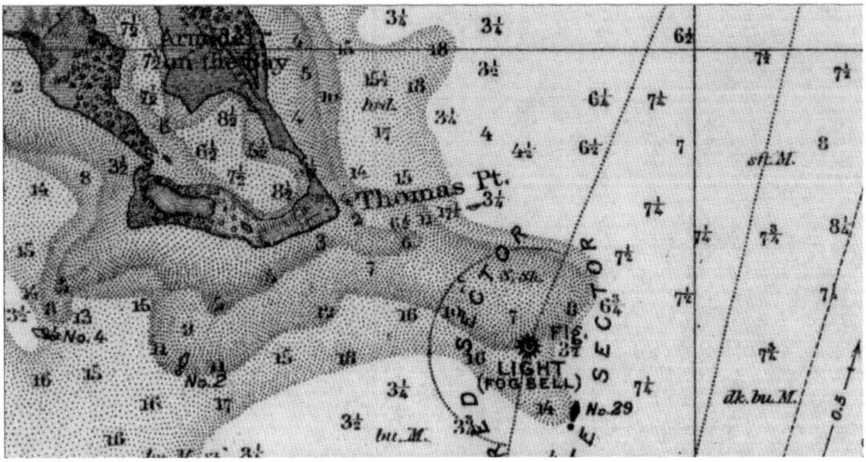

Detail of an 1895 nautical chart showing the Thomas Point Shoal Lighthouse in place and a nearby buoy (no. 29). Note the rapidly shrinking approaches to the tip of the point itself. *U.S. National Archives and Records Administration.*

The second tower collapsed on February 28, 1894, and anything of value that remained at the site was sold at an auction later that year. By 1911, the federal government's plot on the peninsula was down to about an acre and a half and was estimated to be a half mile from the mainland. The federal government began exploring the feasibility of selling of the plot, although the situation was complicated by the shifting sands and the difficulty in determining property lines.

Once what remained of the government's plot was properly defined, it had grown a bit and now measured in at "something about two acres"; a public auction was held at the Annapolis Post Office building on April 1, 1912. The auction was advertised in an Annapolis newspaper and in two Baltimore papers. Eight bidders attended, but only two bid. While the Lighthouse Bureau had privately set its minimum at $2,500, the highest bid was just $350. A subsequent sealed bid auction was held at the Baltimore Custom House and advertised in Annapolis, Baltimore and Washington, D.C., papers. This auction attracted three bidders. Garnett Y. Clark of Ellicott City, Maryland, placed the highest bid at $426 (it was Clark who had bid $350 sixteen months earlier in Annapolis). On January 13, 1914, the Bureau of Lighthouse's Baltimore office recommended to the bureau's Washington, D.C., headquarters that the bid be accepted. The following month, the land was conveyed from the federal government to Clark, and he soon built a bungalow and boathouse at the spot.

In 1928, when responding to an inquiry about the state of his island, Clark reported that the island was now about three acres and "quite dry." Its highest point was about forty feet above the water and was home to about thirty pine trees. While erosion on the south side of his island forced him to move the bungalow, the north side of the island was actually expanding as the sands shifted, causing the area of the property to remain close to steady over his fourteen years of ownership. A powerful 1933 hurricane split the island into two sections. Within the next twenty-five years, all traces of those islands were eroded away. Those who spent summers in nearby Arundel-on-the Bay as late as the 1940s have fond memories of adventures on the islands.

In 1914, the remaining land on the mainland peninsula, to the southwest of the lighthouse site, also passed from federal to private ownership. A few years later, Charles Lee and Ridgley Melvin Sr., both avid sportsmen, sold a seventy-two-acre parcel at the point to the fledgling Thomas Point Duck Club. The club built a small hunting lodge on the property, and a small farm was established, presumably to grow corn to attract waterfowl.

In 1947, the club sold its land to Ferdinand C. and Jane Homer Lee. The Lees recognized a need for public parks and recreational areas in

By 1948, the remaining islands at the tip of Thomas Point are tiny slivers of land. The channel into Fishing Creek has yet to be dredged. The lighthouse shows a flash every five seconds and was equipped with a diaphone fog signal. At this date, the unlit buoy adjacent to the lighthouse was numbered 31. *National Archives and Records Administration.*

Anne Arundel County and, in the early 1960s, sold sections of their land, in four transactions of five dollars each, to Anne Arundel County expressly for this purpose.

Subsequent to the generous gift, a debate unfolded over a number of years regarding the extent of park development appropriate for the land. Residential neighborhoods now lined the access roads, and private homes abutted the county's property at the point. A number of concepts were explored, but in the end, a beautiful but relatively simple forty-five-acre park was created. Parking and facilities are limited at the point, but it is enjoyed on a regular basis by fisherman, picnickers and hikers. The shoreline of the point is now well secured by riprap.

A seven-foot-deep channel was dredged alongside the point in 1970, connecting the Bay with Fishing Creek, which had been a pond when the original towers were built at the point. Now, thanks to ongoing erosion, it connected directly to the Chesapeake at a broad mouth. The channel provided access to a Coast Guard Station planned for the creek. It also opened clear Bay access for dozens of private homes on Thomas Point and in nearby Arundel-on-the-Bay. Remnants of the old point, and the rubble at the foot of the lighthouse, are clearly marked on present-day navigational charts.

1933 HURRICANE AT THOMAS POINT

In mid-August 1933, a powerful hurricane made landfall at North Carolina's Outer Banks and moved up the western shore of the Chesapeake Bay. As it traveled north, the storm, which was later referred to as the "Chesapeake and Potomac Hurricane," wreaked havoc on the Mid-Atlantic. The wind caused nine train cars to blow off the tracks near Washington, D.C. It cut open a new inlet at Ocean City, Maryland, creating the island of Assateague. At Annapolis, it blew out the sandbars at the mouth of Back Creek and caused damage at the United States Naval Academy.

A northerly moving hurricane inland of the Chesapeake Bay's western shore first brings easterly winds to the Bay and then strong southerly winds. An extended period of strong southerlies pushes a massive swell of water up into the upper Bay, where it is penned and continues to rise until the wind subsides. Heavy rainfall over the watershed only serves to increase the rising waters. The 1933 Chesapeake and Potomac Hurricane pushed the water level in the Bay and its tributaries to record heights; many of those records stood for more than seventy years until Hurricane Isabel, which took a track similar to the 1933 storm, pushed the Bay to further heights.

The Chesapeake and Potomac Hurricane had degraded to a tropical storm by the time its center passed just twenty-five miles west of Thomas Point Lighthouse, but the station received a strong blow. Riding out the storm at the lighthouse, and keeping the lamp lit throughout, was Keeper Henry Bryant, a seven-year veteran at Thomas Point, and his longtime assistant, Earl Harris (who was also his son-in-law).

A view, looking northwest, of the Thomas Point Shoal Lighthouse on June 28, 1928. Note the addition, below the cottage, of a storage facility, primarily used to hold coal and wood. *National Archives and Records Administration.*

Bryant and Harris first recorded the approaching storm's easterly wind on the morning of August 23. At the same time, they noted water rising beneath the station. The afternoon's high tide brought the Bay to about four feet of the fuel cellar, positioned underneath the cottage and filled with coal and wood. Later in the day, the wind clocked to the south and increased. As night approached, in the heart of the storm, Bryant and Harris saw spray blowing over the top of their boats, which had been raised above the main-level railing, to the limits of the davits. The Bay continued to rise, and powerful swells marched relentlessly toward the station from the open water to the south. The waves pushed over the stone piles at the base of the lighthouse and moved some of the stones. More troubling was what was happening below the cottage floor. Waves reached the floor of the fuel cellar and carried part of it away, along with some firewood. The coal bin was ripped open, and a large amount of coal (Bryant later estimated between a half ton and a ton) was washed into the Bay.

As the storm lashed at the cottage itself, Bryant and Harris worked tirelessly to keep it intact. "[W]e could not keep the water out of the house," Bryant later reported. "It came in every crease and crack." The pair spent the following day cleaning up and airing out the cottage, and then Henry Bryant wrote out his report for Baltimore. In that letter, which was quickly forwarded to the commissioner of lighthouses in Washington, D.C., he recounted the damage to the fuel cellar and coal bin and the leaking of the cottage and then calmly noted, "No harm done other than that." The storm report closes with two simple but critical sentences: "It did not affect the light. That was excellent." Bryant concluded his report on a dutiful note: "Your anxious to please." A copy of Bryant's letter is on file at the National Archives in Washington, D.C.

Keeper Henry Bryant would go on to serve another six years at the lighthouse. He stepped down in 1939 when the U.S. Coast Guard took over lighthouse operations. All of Bryant's thirteen years of service at the station were alongside Earl Harris, his son-in-law.

LIVING ABOARD

1900s

Despite the beauty all around and the almost constant flow of shipping, the twentieth-century day-to-day life aboard the Thomas Point Shoal screwpile was typically mundane and relatively primitive. When researching a 1979 story, a *Baltimore Sun* reporter located and spoke with Wilson Rawls, a retired Chesapeake Bay lighthouse keeper who lived in the Eastport section of Annapolis. "You had to be pretty independent," he recalled. "We had no electricity, no refrigerator, a kerosene stove and a head out over the balcony. We took our baths in buckets." Rawls told the reporter that as a keeper he sometimes left the station to help extinguish fires on private vessels or pull them off a shallow spot.

The *Sun* reporter spoke with Ella Mae Keagle, also of Eastport, whose father was stationed at Thomas Point in the 1920s. She had spent considerable time at the station as a teenager. She later married a lighthouse keeper and lived at seven lighthouses over thirty-five years. Keagle said, "We had to keep things immaculate, because you never knew when the inspectors would come. We polished the brass, cleaned the lens. For fun we'd go swimming or crabbing. You couldn't be a restless person and you had to know how to entertain yourself." Keagle recalled that when on station, the keeper and his family ate "a lot of cured beef, dried fruit, and canned food. Living was so different then. A lot of rural people lived exactly the same way we did."

In 1934, on-station diesel-powered generators brought electricity to the Thomas Point screwpile, and the lighthouse lamp was converted to electricity the same year.

Above: Thomas Point Shoal Lighthouse, August 2019. *Photo by the author.*

Left: Cypress water cask aboard Thomas Point Shoal Lighthouse, September 2019. This and other casks aboard the lighthouse continue to collect rainwater, which is used, as necessary, in preservation and cleaning projects aboard the lighthouse. *Photo by the author.*

In 1939, the Commerce Department's Lighthouse Service was merged into the United States Coast Guard. The existing Fifth District retained its name and its headquarters at Baltimore. The Coast Guard's Fifth District continues to retain its Baltimore headquarters.

"Ship to shore" radios became prevalent, and Thomas Point was equipped with a unit to communicate with passing ships and shore stations.

The early 1950s saw a major Coast Guard renovation at the Thomas Point Station, including changes to the cottage that were still being addressed in the twenty-first century. The walls in multiple rooms on the primary level were covered with plywood panels. Linoleum tile flooring was installed over the original wood floors. Modern water tanks were installed. A pipe bringing water from shore to the station had been laid across the shoal at an unknown date. A new cable was laid along the shoal connecting the lighthouse to the commercial electrical grid and eliminating the need to frequently run the generators.

In the wake of the technological developments of the Second World War, shipboard electronics advanced dramatically, greatly reducing the number of shipwrecks and groundings, especially in well-charted, well-understood areas such as the Chesapeake Bay. Simultaneously, the gear aboard for aids to navigation, and the buoys themselves, also improved. Floating buoys or pilings driven directly into the Bay's bottom could be topped by strong, predictable onboard lights, eliminating the need for staffing and greatly reducing the need for maintenance. As the twentieth century moved toward its close, the demands of an old screwpile lighthouse—with men to feed, surfaces to paint and infrastructure constantly in need of repair—began to seem like a burden left over from another era. Alternatives were available.

REPRIEVE IN THE 1970s

Throughout the 1960s, the Coast Guard steadily dismantled the Chesapeake's fragile, hard-to-maintain screwpile cottages. In 1966, the 1879 screwpile at Hooper Strait was slated for destruction, and the Eastern Shore community rallied for its preservation. In a bold project, the structure was moved to the fledgling Chesapeake Bay Maritime Museum in St. Michaels, where it remains open to the public. This marked the first organized, successful effort to "save" a Chesapeake screwpile lighthouse, although it involved relocating the structure. The move proved inspirational to those who wanted to preserve the Thomas Point Shoal screwpile.

Eight years after the Hooper Strait structure was moved, the Coast Guard was spending $38,000 per year to staff the Thomas Point Shoal screwpile. The Coast Guard explored the concept of automating and possibly shutting down operations at Thomas Point—perhaps an automated beacon located adjacent to the lighthouse could serve equally as well at a fraction of the cost. Replacing the staff with an automated beacon would only cost $5,000 per year. It seemed that the lighthouse's days as a manned station were numbered, ensuring that its preservation would take strong leadership from the public.

The prospect of change at the lighthouse was met with a strong response from historical, environmental and political groups. Member of Congress Marjorie Holt, elected in 1973 to represent a district that included Annapolis, was the first elected official to learn of the Coast Guard's plans, and she sprang into action, announcing to the press, "The Coast Guard has

Thomas Point Shoal Lighthouse in October 2019 as workers prepare to replace a cracked wooden beam beneath the outdoor privy. *Photo by the author.*

advised me that the old lighthouse will survive only if interested non-profit organizations or local governments agree to maintain and protect it."

Local and regional community leaders heeded the call. Rodney Little, then director of the Baltimore-based Maryland Historic Trust, led the newly formed Lighthouse Foundation Inc., a nonprofit created to preserve historic lighthouses.

In a well-organized and effective bid to draw attention to the situation, in September 1974 Senator Charles Mathias led a flotilla out to the lighthouse including politicians, preservationists, Coast Guard officers and members of the news media. Back at Annapolis, Maryland's Lieutenant Governor Blair Lee held a press conference and announced that if the Coast Guard didn't want the lighthouse, the State of Maryland did.

Throughout the 1970s, broad swaths of rural waterfront along Maryland's western shore were developed into year-round residential communities. These developments often featured community marinas and attracted residents interested in boating and the Chesapeake Bay. The waterfront around Annapolis was among the most highly developed areas. The six-mile route from Annapolis to the Thomas Point peninsula, once primarily open farmland, was by the end of the 1970s highly residential and populated by a large number of citizens who were interested in the health of the Chesapeake Bay and the preservation of its heritage.

Deeply involved in the 1970s efforts was Arthur Sherwood, who had founded the Chesapeake Bay Foundation several years earlier. In 1979, Sherwood said, "It would be a disaster to let Thomas Point go. It is a beautiful and unique structure and with the increasing traffic on the Bay it would seem highly adverse to abandon it."

The overextended Coast Guard continued to view the manned station at Thomas Point as extraneous and noted that advancements in electronic navigation equipment aboard modern ships could help keep them off the shoal. A well-lit, unmanned buoy of appropriate size could effectively replace the aging lighthouse. However, the Coast Guard leadership had learned a lesson from the public outcry; the station at Thomas Point—at least the physical structure—was essentially untouchable. In 1979, a Coast Guard official in Baltimore noted, "These historical societies are pretty powerful, and we won't make a move without arranging it with them ahead of time. It'll be a while before anything happens."

It is important to note that no Coast Guard plans to dismantle the station were brought forward. In fact, it was the Coast Guard, in the midst of the 1974 rallying, that nominated the lighthouse for inclusion in the National Register of Historic Places. A Coast Guard "Realty Specialist," working out of Portsmouth, Virginia, prepared the nomination form. At the time, a Coast Guard official noted wryly, "That fact seems to have gotten lost in the shuffle." If the lighthouse were placed in the National Register, the official noted, "No one can touch the lighthouse, although we could build an automated light next to it."

The Thomas Point Shoal Lighthouse was listed in the National Register of Historic Places in 1975.

THE LAST KEEPERS

"Did you know the Thomas Point lighthouse keepers raise their own food?"
"What? How?"
"Every time the supply boat comes by, they raise up the food from the boat into the lighthouse."
*—attributed to Judge Ridgely P. Melvin Jr. (1917–1999)**

In the 1970s, three Coast Guardsmen were typically assigned to the station. The men worked in two-week-on/one-week-off shifts. While aboard the lighthouse, one of them was awake and on duty at all times. In the early 1970s, Petty Officer Second Class John White, a North Carolina native, became the first African American man to keep the light. White served at Thomas Point for three years and asked for an extension at the end of his tour so he could be in command at the lighthouse during the 100th anniversary of its lighting. The extension was granted, and Thomas Point's first black keeper, by then a petty officer first class, led the lighthouse into its second century. A magazine article profiling White as the centennial keeper noted that he kept in shape by lifting weights and running around the lighthouse twenty-five times in four minutes. White told the writer that he loved the position at Thomas Point and added, "You have a lot of freedom. There's no one to disturb you. It gives you peace of mind and a chance to think a lot."

**Note: The Melvin family owned land at the point in the early twentieth century and large tracts of nearby land along the South River. Judge Melvin liked to tell this joke to guests on his sailboat as they passed the lighthouse. Following his death, Judge Melvin's family and friends spread his ashes in the Chesapeake Bay at Thomas Point.*

John White, a former keeper of the Thomas Point Shoal Lighthouse, during a tour of the lighthouse in 2015. *U.S. Coast Guard photo by Petty Officer Third Class David Marin.*

White's assistant at the time of the article, a twenty-two-year-old from Tennessee named Earnest Taylor, was equally philosophical about his role at Thomas Point and told the reporter, "This light has a lot of values in it....The job makes me feel like I'm doing something important."

Among the keeper's duties in the mid-1970s were keeping the station's logbook and ensuring that the light was operational every day by turning it on a half hour before sunset and then off a half hour after sunrise. The men at the lighthouse called in weather reports to the nearby Coast Guard Station every three hours and, curiously, had an arrangement with a local radio station that required them to call in weather reports every hour from 6:30 a.m. to 7:30 p.m.

John White returned to the lighthouse for a visit in 2015 and pointed out his name, still visible from the main level gallery, carved in the rocks on the north side of the lighthouse.

In late 1979, the *Baltimore Sun* dispatched a reporter to Thomas Point Shoal Lighthouse who filed a story that ran under the headline "Men Pull Lonely Duty at Lighthouse While Need for It Is Debated." The article ran on November 11, 1979, and it provides a glimpse into life aboard the station in the waning years of its full-time occupancy.

The *Sun* was somewhat dismissive of the structure itself and called the lighthouse "[a]n ungainly but quaint anachronism." The opening paragraphs of the article were similarly indifferent about the tasks of the men serving aboard and reported that the lighthouse was "staffed by a rotating crew of four enlisted men whose primary function is to flick a light switch twice a day." However, the article does provide an excellent glimpse into life aboard, and the reporter located two people with decades-old connections to the lighthouse.

In addition to flicking the light switch twice a day, those stationed at Thomas Point were also responsible for activating and deactivating the onboard foghorn, for keeping a log, for reporting station weather conditions over VHF radio and for cleaning the station. When describing how he puts together the visibility portion of the weather reports, one seaman quipped, "It's easy. For visibility, look at the Bay Bridge. If you can see beyond it, it's clear. If you can barely see it, it's hazy."

In 1979, an unrated seaman at the station earned about $600 a month and worked two weeks on and two weeks off. Rated petty officers earned between $800 and $1,100 a month, plus food allowances. A full station inspection took place once a year.

When asked about passing free time at the station, a Coast Guard seaman from Roanoke, Virginia, who, at the time of the reporter's visit, had been at the station for four years, said, "I mostly watch TV, fool around with weights and listen to the radio." Fishing from the lighthouse was also a popular pastime, as was reading magazines and books. Upon visiting the station, the *Sun* reporter noted "neat stacks of Playboy magazines, a color TV, and a shelf of paperback novels." The seaman added, "Anyone with an attitude won't make it out here."

A young Coast Guard man stationed at Thomas Point was blunt with the reporter: "[I]t gets a little lonely, but it's secluded too. You can slack off, grow a beard, and there is no one looking over your shoulder."

Through the 1970s and into the 1980s, local recreational boaters continued the longstanding tradition of delivering food and books to the station. A water desalinator was installed in 1981, and a video game system was brought to the lighthouse shortly thereafter.

In 1984, the second-to-last holiday season at the manned lighthouse, a three-foot-high Christmas tree was lit inside the cottage, and members of the Coast Guard Auxiliary worked shifts aboard the lighthouse so its keepers could spend the holiday with their families.

AUTOMATION IN THE 1980s

Pressed by tight budgets and lack of manpower, the Coast Guard remained eager to move personnel off the lighthouse and into other roles. At the dawn of the 1980s, it was costing the Coast Guard $60,000 a year to man and maintain the lighthouse. In March 1980, the Coast Guard carefully announced that it planned to take its men off the station and automate the horn and light. The automated lighthouse would remain in place and under Coast Guard care. The actual transition to automation was still several years away, the service noted, but being aware of public sentiment, it wanted to get the word out early.

By the spring of 1984, with its men still serving aboard the station, the Coast Guard actively searched for a civilian caretaker to live aboard the station. Dozens of applications were received, but the plan never came to fruition. It was not until September 5, 1986, that the Thomas Point Shoal screwpile was automated and officially un-manned. As the Coast Guard prepared to leave the station in the hands of the automated equipment, a service official noted, "Maybe we've become what the caboose became for the railroad. God knows we love our cabooses."

The automation was featured in a front-page story in Annapolis's *Evening Capital* newspaper. The article called the cottage "slightly eccentric" while noting that even as the station's last Coast Guard keeper departed the lighthouse, the new automated equipment was malfunctioning, "sounding the foghorn for no apparent reason."

The acrylic lens atop Thomas Point Shoal Lighthouse sits atop the original cast-iron base. *Photo by the author.*

Even as the automation took place, harbingers of Thomas Point Shoal Lighthouse's life beyond the Coast Guard began to emerge. The *Evening Capital* article on the automation mentioned nonprofits getting involved in helping preserve the lighthouse and opening it to public access of some kind. The idea of a bed-and-breakfast was also discussed.

The lighthouse's Fourth Order Fresnel lens, installed in 1899 and valued at $1.5 million by 1986, was removed as part of the automation process. It now resides in Coast Guard offices at Curtis Bay near Baltimore. Today, an acrylic lens and battery-powered bulb operate together in the Thomas Point station's lantern room, placed atop the original cast-iron and brass pedestal.

While a new beacon, foghorn and weather reading gear continued to operate aboard the lighthouse, the automated structure itself simply became a vessel to hold that equipment. To protect against vandalism, bulletproof thermoplastic windows replaced glass, and an alarm was installed. The Coast Guard continued to maintain the lighthouse, while simultaneously, ashore, various groups floated concepts around preservation and uses for the screwpile. Aside from maintaining the active equipment, exterior and basic structure, the Coast Guard essentially left the interior of the cottage untouched. Eighteen years later, when the City of Annapolis and its partners took possession, they found the interior resembled a time capsule from September 1986.

STRUCTURE, CURRENT AND DEPTH

FISH AT THOMAS POINT

The quality and composition of the water over the shoal and around the lighthouse are affected by storms, droughts and humans, but even as the world above the beacon and around it evolves, the Thomas Point shoreline, shoal and lighthouse base remain an extremely attractive environment for fish. Over centuries, some types of fish have maintained a constant presence at the shoal, while other species mysteriously appear at Thomas Point, thrive and then fade away. One constant, however, beginning centuries before Captain John Smith first explored the area, is the presence of fishermen at the point and over the shoal.

The initial primary targets for colonial anglers at Thomas Point were Atlantic sturgeons; prized for their meat and eggs, they are the Chesapeake Bay's largest native fish. The Chesapeake Bay sturgeon harvest peaked in 1890s, when more than 700,000 pounds were caught. After decades of aggressive overfishing, that catch had been reduced by more than 90 percent by the 1920s. The Atlantic sturgeon fishery is currently closed on the Chesapeake and along the East Coast of the United States.

Ask a lifelong Chesapeake angler such as Lenny Rudow about fishing in a particular location, and the conversation quickly turns to the cycles of fish population and resident species. Schools of fish grow and shrink. Unexpected species make surprise appearances and abrupt departures. Some of these cycles are created by natural events such as storms, moon cycles and water flow, while others are influenced by pressures from anglers and managed by regulators. Most frequently, population cycles occur, and species simply and unpredictably arrive and depart as if driven by unknown forces. "Mankind just doesn't know what makes some of it happen the way it happens," Rudow said with a shrug of the shoulders. "It just happens and the fishermen react to it."

Lenny Rudow first visited Thomas Point as a boy in the 1970s aboard his family's small powerboat. At the time, the Chesapeake's striped bass population was severely depleted, and Rudow's target at the shoal was bluefish. "I was a young boy and remember running down from Baltimore to chase bluefish at Thomas Point." Now a fishing author and closely followed expert, Rudow continues to be a steady presence in Thomas Point fishery.

When asked what species he and other anglers have caught at Thomas Point in the past few decades, Rudow reeled off an impressive list, including bluefish, flounder, striped bass, seabass, Spanish mackerel, white perch, spot, croaker, speckled trout, blue catfish, channel catfish, cobia and red drum. One logical connection to the arrival and departure of certain species at the shoal is the salinity level of the water over it. In dry years, with salinity levels high at the shoal, Rudow has caught salt water–loving seabass and red drum in the shadow of the lighthouse. Tarpon have been found in nearby fishing nets. Other years, after storms and heavy rainfall turn the Bay water fresher, Rudow has hooked blue catfish in the same waters.

Other species arrive and depart with less obvious reason. Rudow recalled, "In the early 1990s, flounder started showing up there, and they were there for about ten years. Thomas Point was a flounder hotspot; they were all over the shoal. Flounder probably peaked there around the turn of this century, and then they began disappearing. They're gone now." He also recalled massive schools of the shy weakfish lurking in the deeper cool water at a sharp drop-off just north of the lighthouse. Then the weakfish, like the flounder, slowly and then suddenly disappeared.

As the weakfish and flounder came and went, other species have arrived and thrived. "We are having a Spanish mackerel run right now that is the best in my lifetime," Rudow said. As Rudow spoke in the late summer of 2019, white perch, spot and croaker were all found in large numbers at Thomas Point. According to Rudow, the diverse Thomas Point fishery thrives because it offers three key elements of a vibrant underwater ecosystem: structure, current and depth.

Structure is the underwater physical material on the shoal, including the rocks under the lighthouse, the steel of the lighthouse supports and the icebreaker on the north side of the lighthouse base. "Fish love the ecosystem around underwater structure....Little critters grow on that structure—mussels and the barnacles and that sort of thing—it starts the whole food web. And then the crabs come in and then the smaller fish come in and there it is."

Rudow noted that the relatively strong currents running over the shoal and around the lighthouse are also attractive to fish. "You get a tremendous rush of water over that shoal," he said. "When it is running hard, it can stir things up and dislodge those little critters. It stirs up the bottom. As a rule of thumb, moving water generally generates more action than non-moving water."

According to Rudow, the variety of depth around the point and shoal provides options for feeding fish. "This allows the fish to group up in different depths depending on sunlight and time of day," he said. "The bigger fish like to feed on the rocks in shallow water near the shoreline. But in the middle of a bright summer sunny day, you're not going to find a fish in the shallow water. They don't want to be that exposed. They head out to deeper, darker water."

Structure and moving water in a variety of depths are all found at Thomas Point. As a result, Thomas Point attracts massive schools of fish that, in turn, attract anglers from Baltimore to Solomons and everywhere in between. Rudow called the area including the Thomas Point Shoal and the lighthouse a top-ten fishing hotspot on the Chesapeake Bay.

Rudow has seen up to fifty boats at the lighthouse and on the shoal. At any given time, a subset of them are jockeying for position close to the structure at the base of the lighthouse. "Only five or six boats can really fish up against the lighthouse before it becomes a complete disaster," he said. With a mix of professional captains running large boats full of paying guests and recreational fishermen in smaller boats, tensions can occasionally get high. "In the old days, they used to throw lead weights at each other's boats. I don't think that happens any more, but there has been some shouting when a lot of boats all try to push in close to the lighthouse."

The crowds on the water at Thomas Point are typically fishing for striped bass. Any conversation with a Chesapeake Bay fisherman naturally turns to striped bass, known locally as "rockfish" and as "stripers." Striped bass are tasty, beloved and heavily fished on the Chesapeake Bay and at Thomas Point.

Like the fabled sturgeon before them, the striped bass have been a popular targets for decades. Today, with advanced communication methods and modern fishing technology so widely available, the striped bass population

Annapolis watermen working crab pots on the Thomas Point Shoal, September 2019. *Photo by the author.*

is targeted very effectively and by a large number of anglers. As a result, the fishery is closely managed, monitored and regulated.

Some of the biggest rockfish are found right at the rocks below the lighthouse, hence the crush of boats pressing close. Those rocks are also sharp, jagged and prone to snag an errantly cast lure. When asked how many snagged and broken-off lures are on the rocks beneath the lighthouse, Lenny Rudow laughed and said, "Somewhere between 30 and 50 million. Me and the people on my boat probably lose a hundred jigs a year there."

When asked to predict the future of the Thomas Point fishery, Lenny Rudow smiled and said, "It's totally impossible to tell, and I try not to be in the prediction business. But the one thing I will say is that there will always be a fishery there. And as long there are rockfish, rockfish will love it at Thomas Point."

In addition to the gamefish pursued by Lenny Rudow and hundreds of other anglers, a diverse ecosystem thrives at the shoal and around the lighthouse. Among other critters, one can find blue crabs, oysters, clams and horseshoe crabs on the bottom. Occasional sightings of bottlenose dolphins, cownose rays, sharks and even a lost manatee filter in every few years. Eels, menhaden, alewife herring, needlefish, spot and a variety of small minnows and baitfish also populate Thomas Point Shoal waters.

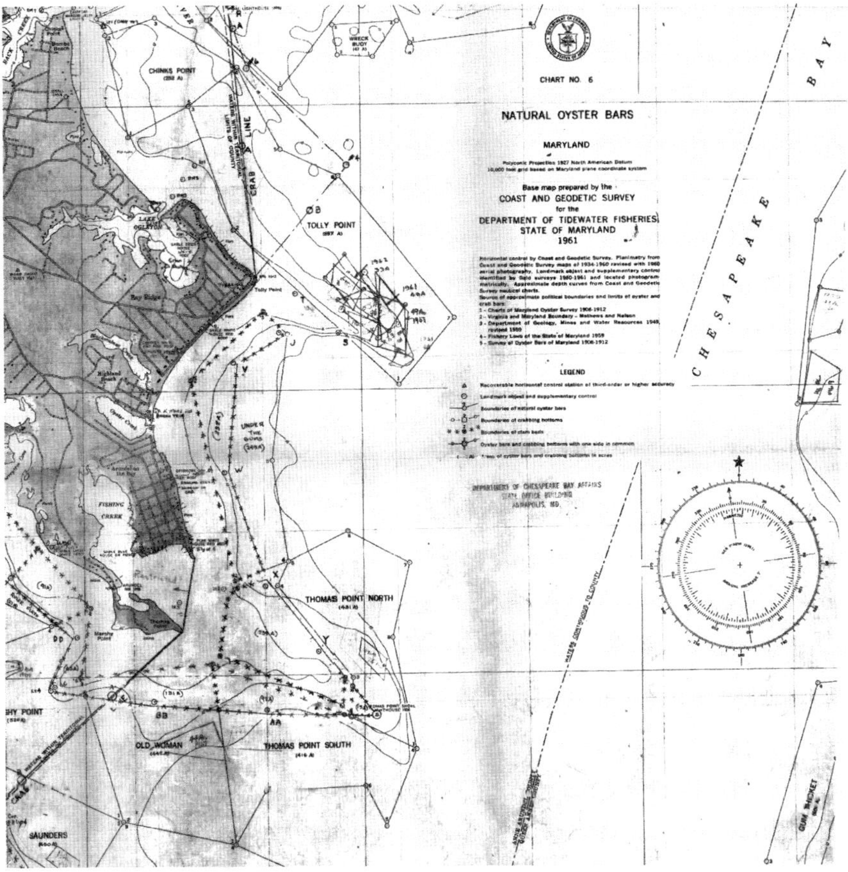

A 1961 chart of natural oyster bars in the vicinity of Thomas Point Shoal. *National Archives and Records Administration.*

MUCH LIKE IT WAS in mid-nineteenth-century ship's offices on the docks at Baltimore, in the late twentieth century a reliable and talented sailor could find rewarding work that would deliver him to waterways all around the planet.

By his late twenties, Tom Weaver, an affable and articulate sailor of indeterminate English and Antipodal origins, had logged thousands of miles racing grand prix yachts alongside some of the world's wealthiest sportsmen. The services of sailors with Weaver's skill set and attitude were always in demand, although they now worked on the decks of racing sailboats and in sun-kissed destinations. Weaver worked aboard the race boats off the coasts of Italy and France, in the trade winds off Hawaii and across the Caribbean. On a sunny morning in 1991, he was on the waters off of Annapolis, sailing in his first race on the brackish Chesapeake Bay. Carrying a wide breadth of experiences, Weaver was not expecting any surprises on the relatively inland race course.

"Almost all of the sailing we had been doing up to that point was in deep water," Weaver recalled with a smile. "Even if there are rocks or islands, the water drops right off and is deep immediately. It was quite shocking to be sailing along off Annapolis, focused on the boat and the race, and suddenly there is a shoal out into the center of the Bay—no way could you try to cross it…and there is this odd lighthouse on the end of it, right in the middle of the course. I had never seen anything like it."

Shortly after seeing Thomas Point for the first time, Weaver moved to Annapolis, which had become an attractive permanent base for international racing sailors. He continued to work in the sailing industry, logging time on America's Cup and 'round-the-world race teams and coaching other top sailors. Along the way, he was introduced to the challenge of fishing for Chesapeake striped bass from the decks of small boats, using light tackle. In 2000, Weaver coached a pair of teams at the Star Class World Championship, which was hosted by the Annapolis Yacht Club and contested on the Chesapeake. During one race, as the fleet passed Thomas Point on a three-mile leg, Weaver cast a fishing line off the stern of his coach boat. Almost instantaneously, he hooked into a sizeable striped bass. As the Star Class fleet streamed by, Weaver brought the fish to the boat. As Weaver boated the fish, the nearby Australian team coaches stared on in disbelief. Back ashore, when Weaver's friends heard this story, they simply nodded and smiled. They already knew that this sailor was hooked on fishing.

Twenty years later, Tom Weaver continues to work in the marine industry, racing, building boats and consulting on projects, but over the years, the fishing came to consume more of his time and energy. Weaver studied, absorbed and logged ten thousand hours on small boats with lines out. Although he simultaneously manages multiple other professional projects, Weaver is deeply committed to the business he has built as a licensed Chesapeake Bay fishing guide, working out of Eastport. All the skills he honed as a professional racing sailor—the preparation; the tactics; a deep understanding of weather, gear and geography; and a genuine engagement with the clients—are now focused on light tackle fishing on the Chesapeake Bay and its tributaries. Weaver is sponsored by brands he believes in, and he is constantly in demand; some clients fly thousands of miles for a session fishing with him. Tom Weaver is on or near Thomas Point Shoal more than one hundred days a year.

Fishing guide Tom Weaver and a healthy striped bass caught and released back into the Chesapeake Bay at the Thomas Point Shoal Lighthouse, October 2019. *Photo by the author.*

Fishing guide Tom Weaver and clients pursue striped bass at the Thomas Point Shoal Lighthouse, September 2019. *Photo by the author.*

A fishing session alongside Tom Weaver at Thomas Point is like looking inside the brain of an ace major-league pitcher in the heat of an important inning. Before giving his clients the okay to cast, Weaver takes in a dozen external signals—current, wind, water surface, nearby birds, faraway birds, water temperature, depth, positions of nearby boats, electronic blots on his fish finder and chatter on his cellphone and VHF radio—and measures all of this alongside the vast personal experience he has recorded, as well as the experiences of others he has gleaned along the way. Weaver moves carefully and thoughtfully, but he moves with a true purpose. Every cast matters.

By October, the waters at the Thomas Point Shoal churn with thousands of undersized striped bass, all hungry and eager to race after shiny bits of metal and plastic. While hooking into these young fish is relatively easy and can be entertaining, Weaver makes a real effort to avoid doing so. Catch-and-release fishing can be damaging to a fish, especially if executed carelessly. Fishermen frequently report catching rockfish with damaged mouths from multiple encounters with fishhooks; repeat customers—they just won't learn. Weaver brings a conservationist mindset to his fishing, sometimes even clashing with his friends in the sportfishing industry who favor less restrictive proposals for managing the Chesapeake striped bass ecosystem. For Tom Weaver, catching undersized fish is more than a disappointment—it is something like a defeat, especially when he knows there are bigger fish below.

Beneath the school of juveniles, in darker, colder water, are the keepers. Tom Weaver has developed a special knack for finding them. The deeper fish are wiser, heavier and more careful. On a good day, when he is in the vicinity of the big fish, Weaver won't sanction a cast from his boat until he has confidence that the big ones are near the boat and that he has a logistical approach to hooking them. On slower days—and no fisherman who ever lived doesn't have slow days—he keeps moving while calculating and evolving the strategy of his pursuit. There are no wasted minutes and no wasted casts.

Although the majority of his fishing is catch and release, the striped bass are tasty and treasured ashore. If the keepers are biting, Weaver will happily guide his clients to their legal limit and then, back at the pier, filet the fish for them.

In large part, the Thomas Point fishery works, Weaver said, because of its unique geography, extending at a ninety-degree angle to the current. This constant flow in and out of the Bay, over various depths, hosts an attractive food chain, with striped bass near, but not quite at, its apex. The structure, the moving water and the varied bottom depths are consistent themes of Thomas Point mentioned by the top area's fishermen.

Weaver went on to explain that Thomas Point's spot on the map, within easy reach of dozens of professional charter fishing boats and accessible by a thousand or more powerboats run by recreational fishermen, puts constant pressure on the shoal and the area around the lighthouse. Despite the pressure, it is just too good. The fish are there. When it's working, the fast spread of information on social media only attracts more fishermen.

And when it's not working? "If the client has caught his limit or if things are very slow and we just need to get our heads out of the boat for a moment, everyone loves a close pass by the lighthouse," Weaver said. "The phones come out for photos, and it just makes everyone happy. I have seen that lighthouse thousands of times, and it still makes me smile. It's sort of magical."

TRANSITION AT THOMAS POINT

Steadfast, serene, immovable, the same
Year after year, through all the silent night
Burns on forevermore that quenchless flame,
Shines on that inextinguishable light!
—Henry Wadsworth Longfellow, "The Lighthouse," 1849

By the turn of the twenty-first century, the now automated Thomas Point Shoal Lighthouse had outlived its practicality as an active, federally owned station. In conjunction with the U.S. Coast Guard, the federal government's General Services Administration declared Thomas Point Shoal Lighthouse "excess to the needs of the United States of America." Thomas Point was not the only historic lighthouse subject to this stark reality. Dozens of other historic lighthouses around the country were reaching the same point in their lifespans: too historic to tear down but too needy to manage and maintain with federal resources.

While the federal government was keen to divest itself of its old lighthouses, it was also eager to see the most historic among them properly preserved. The National Lighthouse Preservation Act of 2000 included a concept designed to ensure the future of Thomas Point Shoal Lighthouse and similar structures. Any transfer of a historic lighthouse out of government hands would fall under the purview of the Lighthouse Preservation Act. A program was developed to facilitate no-cost transfer of qualified lighthouses to other government agencies or to nonprofit

Thomas Point Shoal Lighthouse, September 2019. *Photo by the author.*

organizations. The spirit of the act was to allow well-vetted government agencies (federal, state, local) and nonprofits to own, maintain and operate historic lighthouses for the public benefit.

The government's General Services Administration works alongside the Coast Guard and the National Park Service in the transfer of historic lighthouses under the program. In the fall of 2002, Thomas Point Shoal Lighthouse was one of nineteen lighthouses listed as available for transfer to qualified applicants.

Recognizing the unique situation at Thomas Point, the United States Lighthouse Society, a nonprofit organization dedicated to America's historic lighthouses, sprang into action. The society's leadership began the application process and quickly partnered with the City of Annapolis, the Annapolis Maritime Museum and Anne Arundel County. Annapolis mayor

Ellen Moyer and city leaders recognized that while the city itself was in a strong position to assume ownership of the lighthouse, it was in no position to run or maintain the structure—tasks that required additional funding and resources, as well as deep expertise. The Lighthouse Society could nicely fill this operational role, and its efforts would be augmented by the wholehearted support of the fledgling Annapolis Maritime Museum, whose leaders and volunteers were eager to get deeply involved in the day-to-day operations of the lighthouse and help organize fundraising efforts.

It was quickly determined that the consortium's proposal would feature an arrangement in which the city held the deed to the lighthouse and, simultaneously, held a long-term, no-cost lease agreement with the U.S. Lighthouse Society and its Chesapeake chapter. The society would act as the city's "operations agent" at the lighthouse. The society also assumed financial responsibility. The lease term was thirty years with two thirty-year extension options.

Henry Gonzalez, president of the Chesapeake Bay chapter of the U.S. Lighthouse Society, was instrumental in putting together the proposal and was justifiably optimistic about its structure and participants. "We were confident from the beginning," he later noted.

In December 2003, the Annapolis City Council passed the associated legislation, and the lease was drawn up before the group's application was even approved by the federal government. As Gonzalez knew, the group's case was strong, and once submitted to the federal government, the proposed arrangement was impossible to ignore.

One irony of the new arrangement is that Thomas Point itself is several miles outside of the city's borders. The Annapolis city government, its namesake maritime museum and the community's leaders had stepped up to preserve a lighthouse that had been built by the federal government at behest of Baltimore on land originally owned by the State of Maryland. The bold move by Annapolis would have been impossible without the leadership and support of the U.S. Lighthouse Society, which continued to deliver the energy, expertise and labor to properly manage and preserve the lighthouse.

THE TRANSFER CEREMONY

As hoped, the administrators of the transfer program approved the group's application, and on the sunny Saturday morning of May 1, 2004, hundreds

Annapolis mayor Ellen Moyer at the 2004 ceremony marking the handover of the Thomas Point Shoal Lighthouse from the federal government to the City of Annapolis. Moyer was instrumental in the process and continued to be a strong advocate for preservation of the lighthouse, even after leaving office. *U.S. National Archives and Records Administration.*

gathered at the Annapolis City Dock, where a Thomas Point Lighthouse transfer ceremony headlined the Annapolis Maritime Heritage Festival. Although the official legal documents were still in development, this was a done deal, and all sides were thrilled with the outcome and the potential.

Gale Norton, President George W. Bush's secretary of the interior, represented the federal government at the ceremony and was ebullient in her praise of the local effort. From the podium, Norton said that the lighthouse "symbolizes much more than its past and its historical significance of the last lighthouse of its kind…it symbolizes the kind of private and public partnerships that will protect historic, cultural and national treasures for the future."

Ellen Moyer, Annapolis's first female mayor and a dedicated supporter of maritime heritage, represented the city and was described in media accounts as "ecstatic" with the new arrangement.

Joining Norton and Moyer on stage were Annapolis Maritime Museum president L.B. "Buck" Buchanan, U.S. Lighthouse Society president Wayne Wheeler, U.S. Coast Guard rear admiral Sally Brice-O'Hara and Barbara Shelton, who represented the federal government's General Services Administration. David Gendell, author of this book, served as the host and emcee of the historic ceremony.

Two grandsons of former Thomas Point Shoal Lighthouse keeper John Suit were on hand for the ceremony. Suit was active on area lighthouses in the late nineteenth and early twentieth centuries and served as keeper from 1904 into 1908. Suit's eventful term at Thomas Point is described elsewhere in this book.

NEW LIFE AT THOMAS POINT

I think every volunteer who works on this lighthouse and other lighthouses have their own stories and connections. I do think it's important to transfer this sense of history from generation to generation.
—Bob Stevenson, longtime volunteer at Thomas Point Shoal Lighthouse

Several weeks after the transfer ceremony, on July 23, 2004, the federal government officially signed over the deed to the lighthouse to the City of Annapolis. Mayor Ellen Moyer signed the transfer document and accepted the property on behalf of the city. The transfer was made "without monetary consideration," although there are stipulations in its body designed to preserve both the structure and government access to it.

Before construction of the lighthouse began, the State of Maryland signed over the bottomland under it to the federal government in October 1874. More than a century later, the federal government wanted to hold on to its bit of Chesapeake Bay bottom, and the 2004 document explicitly stated that it was only the lighthouse itself being transferred. The bottomland under it would be retained by the federal government. The precise working of the deed noted that "no submerged lands shall be conveyed by this instrument."

The deed also noted the specific latitude and longitude of the center of the lighthouse and that the boundary line of the transferred property extends 263.3 feet from the center in every direction. No shoreside property was conveyed with the deed (the land on the actual tip of the point is now owned by Anne Arundel County and is public park land).

Thomas Point Shoal Lighthouse, September 2018. *Photo by the author.*

While the federal government was ready to get the station off its books and had found ideal partners to pass it on to, its agencies still desired access to the station. This access was written into the transfer document. In conjunction with the deed transfer, the U.S. Department of Commerce (acting on behalf of the National Oceanic and Atmospheric Administration, the scientific agency under its purview) secured "permission to use the Light Station for installation, maintenance and operation of a Coastal Marine Automated Network weather package." This particular use was considered an aid to navigation, and as such, NOAA coordinated its use with the U.S. Coast Guard.

The Coast Guard was granted both unrestricted access to the property and the right to continue to use the site in the service of navigation. The Coast Guard had the right to enter the property at any time for the purpose of maintaining the aids to navigation and the associated equipment, but it had to give the new owners prior notice of visits. The new owners were barred from interfering with the navigational aids on the site without receiving written permission first. The Coast Guard also retained the right to access the station for the purpose of rehabilitating the property as necessary to fulfill its mission as a navigational aid.

A crew from Coast Guard Station Annapolis shuttle members of the Coast Guard Aids to Navigation Team Baltimore to Thomas Point Shoal Lighthouse aboard its forty-one-foot utility boat in 2011. *U.S. Coast Guard photo by Petty Officer Third Class Robert Brazzell.*

Petty Officer First Class Justin Blais of the Coast Guard Aids to Navigation Team Baltimore troubleshoots electrical equipment on the Thomas Point Shoal Lighthouse in 2011. *U.S. Coast Guard photo by Petty Officer Third Class Robert Brazzell.*

Petty Officer Second Class Lee Currier of the Coast Guard Aids to Navigation Team Baltimore inspects the lighting equipment of the Thomas Point Shoal Lighthouse in 2011. *U.S. Coast Guard photo by Petty Officer Third Class Robert Brazzell.*

The property is in the National Register of Historic Places, and in Maryland, such properties are administered by the Maryland Historical Trust, a state agency. Responsibility for all covenants regarding maintaining and preserving the lighthouse's "historic features" was conveyed to the new owners.

Shortly after the transfer ceremony, renowned lighthouse preservationist Cullen Chambers developed a comprehensive plan for preserving the Thomas Point Shoal Lighthouse. Henry Gonzalez from the Lighthouse Society emerged as a boots-on-the-ground leader and began the hard work of managing the station's preservation.

The new caretaker's first steps at the station were tentative. Back in September 2003, Hurricane Isabel had destroyed the lighthouse's wooden dock, rendering access difficult and major repair efforts impossible. The same storm caused severe damage at the Annapolis Maritime Museum's headquarters in an old oyster processing facility on Back Creek at Annapolis. Museum leaders were now doubly challenged by rebuilding a damaged headquarters and helping restore a lighthouse. The Coast Guard assumed responsibility for lighthouse dock project (the station was, at the time of the storm, under federal ownership). As they waited for the Coast Guard to arrive and make the repairs, Gonzalez and other eager volunteers were limited in their access to the station.

In the long months that passed while they awaited the rebuilt access dock, the new owners of the lighthouse stayed active. Ellen Moyer, Buck Buchanan and others organized fundraisers and drummed up support ashore, bolstering the budget. Fresh grant applications were made, and in response, two enthusiastic area nonprofits, the Four Rivers Heritage Area and Preservation Maryland, made early grants to help fund the initial architectural and engineering assessments of the structure.

Finally, in May 2005, the Coast Guard completed the dock repairs, and major preservation efforts could begin. Once the dock was replaced and access reestablished, Henry Gonzalez and a crew of volunteers began an ambitious preservation and restoration process. Gonzalez and others kept a meticulous timeline of the early work at the lighthouse.

The first work crew arrived at the Thomas Point screwpile on August 8, 2005. Cleaning up and assessing the situation at the station was an initial priority, and most of the volunteers spent those early days scrubbing down the cottage. Other volunteers began removing the Coast Guard's kitchen cabinets and appliances, as well as twentieth-century flooring and plywood.

The Getty Foundation, the National Park Service's Chesapeake Bay Gateways Program and the Maryland Historical Trust each delivered generous grants aimed at restoring the screwpile foundation above the waterline, building an expanded dock and addressing other important items on the work list.

By 2006, the landing dock was expanded, lead paint issues were addressed, rotten decking and siding were replaced and a lightning protection system was installed. The major issue of restoring the structural foundation still loomed over the project. The structural work was specialized and expensive. A contractor was secured, but one week into their structural work, one of the contractor's barges came loose and damaged the steel supports under the lighthouse. The damaged steel was replaced by the contractor. Work was soon halted due to winter weather. The difficulty in securing a qualified contractor, the associated expenses, the barge incident and the weather delay all foreshadowed the ongoing challenges of maintaining the screwpile foundation. The project was completed in mid-2007, aided greatly by the leadership of U.S. Lighthouse Society volunteer Tom McCracken.

In 2007, the Annapolis Maritime Museum ramped up its tour operations, with twenty-five trained docents and a contracted boat and captain. Tours began in midsummer, and many were sold out. By year's end, hundreds of people had visited the lighthouse as part of the program.

Over the course of 2007, windows, doors and cedar shutters were replaced under the watchful eye of the Maryland Historical Trust, which ensured historical accuracy. Much of the material was donated by supportive businesses, and a great deal of labor was put forth by Lighthouse Society volunteers. Underpinning the donated material and labor were grants from interested organizations. Baltimore's France-Merrick Foundation made a grant to restore the roof. The Maryland Historical Trust came through again with funding for ongoing structural support restoration.

The four rooms on the primary level were approached thoughtfully, and the attention to detail is remarkable. One is a sitting room representing the lighthouse in the late nineteenth century, shortly after it opened, and includes period furniture. The kitchen is also set up in a way it would have been in the nineteenth century, including a waffle iron and a Lighthouse Service place setting of dishes. In 2013, volunteers hoisted aboard an eighty-pound potbelly stove that had been carefully restored by volunteer Hobie Statzer. Three years later, a nineteenth-century stove that had been purchased and restored by Statzer was placed in the kitchen. Statzer ably served the lighthouse for more than a decade and brought great passion and expertise to the preservation effort.

The room serving as the Coast Guard workroom was re-created to match photographs from the era, including a pair of clocks, one on Greenwich Mean Time and one on local time. The room is set to look as it did in 1986, when the last keepers manned the station. Cathy Lewis, a tireless volunteer at the lighthouse, found a 1970s SHARP television that exactly matched a set pictured in a period photograph and placed it in the room in the same spot as shown in the photograph.

After seeing a photograph of a bookshelf that was taken in the final year of the Coast Guard crews aboard the lighthouse, Henry Gonzalez combed bookstores and eBay and was able to secure the exact books on the shelf. They are now placed on the bookshelf in the same order they are pictured in the period photo.

The fourth room on the primary level that once contained the Coast Guard generator is now used for storage and equipment used by preservationists. At the time of a 2019 visit, the room included a tool chest, a table saw, a portable generator and other supplies. There is no standard electrical power at the lighthouse, as it was removed in the 1986 Coast Guard automation process.

The galley aboard Thomas Point Shoal Lighthouse has been carefully renovated to a state reflecting what it might have looked like in 1875. *Photo by the author.*

The workroom aboard Thomas Point Shoal Lighthouse has been carefully renovated to reflect what it looked like in the final years of the Coast Guard era, including flooring, paint and furniture. This room was originally a bedroom. *Photo by the author.*

Solar panels atop the Thomas Point Shoal Lighthouse, September 2019. *Photo by the author.*

The second floor served as a dormitory area in the Coast Guard era and is largely open. It was on this level that former keeper John White showed visitors where his bunk had been located, in an alcove, beneath a dormer. In 2018 and 2019, volunteers pulled up orange tile flooring on this level and exposed the original yellow pine floor. The wooden floor has since been restored. A display of nineteenth-century keeper equipment, including brass containers used to carry kerosene up to the lamp, is on one side of the second level. A hand-cranked fog bell, used prior to 1939, is on the other side. The current foghorn was run by the station's batteries, which are connected to solar panels. However, extended periods of fog bell use drained the battery bank to the point that their ability to power the light was compromised, so the fog bell was discontinued in 2017.

Shoreside, volunteers researched historic records of the station and made contact with descendants of former keepers. Researchers contacted an eighth-great-grandson of Phillip Thomas, the namesake of the point. Among the first volunteers stepping forward to devote time, energy and expertise to the lighthouse was Howard Lewis, the great-grandson of Charles W. Hartmann, who served as a keeper aboard the lighthouse from 1898 to 1901. Lewis's family has been based in the Eastport section of Annapolis since the 1870s. Howard and his wife, Cathy, have devoted

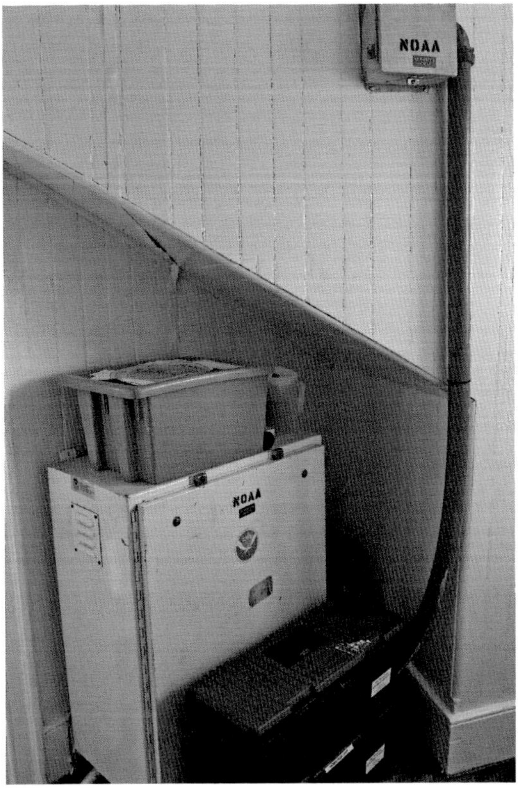

Right: Weather reporting equipment owned and maintained by the National Oceanographic and Atmospheric Administration aboard Thomas Point Shoal Lighthouse, September 2019. *Photo by the author.*

Below: The four twelve-volt batteries powering the light at Thomas Point Shoal Lighthouse, September 2019. The batteries are charged with solar power. *Photo by the author.*

Since 2004, Howard and Cathy Lewis have logged countless hours in the preservation of Thomas Point Shoal Lighthouse. *Photo by the author.*

countless hours to the preservation of the lighthouse. The majority of the visitor and work trips to the lighthouse have been enabled by Lewis and his workboat, *Audacious*.

The preservation work continued unabated. Some sessions featured more than a dozen volunteers, often from the Chesapeake chapter of the U.S. Lighthouse Society. Their work sessions are well documented and reflect a remarkable level of effort. The logs describe "the never-ending sanding and painting of walls and doors and well, just about anything that isn't moving." Notes from one productive day in 2013 report that "[v]olunteers were all over the light."

Over the fifteen years since it was handed over by the government, the Thomas Point screwpile has buzzed with activity, but there are long stretches with no human activity aboard. The roof and railings of the vacant cottage became a popular gathering point for seagulls and other birds. In an effort to keep the birds off the structure, volunteers researched, purchased and installed a pair of bird repellant audio systems. Solar panels power batteries that enable broadcast of loud recordings featuring "gulls in distress." One audio broadcast unit is mounted on the gallery of the primary level and the other on the lantern level. The recordings do not keep the birds away entirely, but they do minimize their visits.

THE LIGHTHOUSE TODAY

It will never stop. We are going to constantly have to be out here involved with the lighthouse.
—John Potwin, longtime volunteer at Thomas Point Shoal Lighthouse and preservation foreman for the 2019–20 restoration projects

Tours, research and preservation work have continued at the lighthouse, but not without setbacks. In mid-April 2016, vandals boarded the lighthouse and wreaked havoc. It is believed that the intruders rappelled up to the lantern-level gallery. They then used the twelve-volt battery that powered a bird repellent speaker to smash a glass pane and enter the lantern room. From there, they descended into the lighthouse cottage, breaking windows and discharging fire extinguishers along the way. In the incident, a number of the iconic wooden balusters were destroyed. The 1970s-era television, placed in the lighthouse to match the set featured in a photograph during the Coast Guard's final years on the station, was smashed on the rocks below the cottage. Annapolis Maritime Museum executive director Alice Estrada estimated the monetary damage at $15,000, but also noted that the labor devoted to the lighthouse by volunteers, many of whom were elderly, was difficult to replace. The public outcry was fierce and media coverage extensive, but the vandals have not been located.

Howard Lewis, the great-grandson of a keeper, and his wife, Cathy, were the first to arrive at the lighthouse after the incident and discovered the damage. The Lewises climbed onto the rocks and collected the smashed

A 1970s-era television in the workroom at the Thomas Point Shoal Lighthouse. It matches a set seen in period photographs of the lighthouse interior. In 2016, it was smashed by vandals and recovered from the rocks below by lighthouse volunteers. *Photo by the author.*

parts of the set. As the cleanup took place, the Lewises carefully glued the television back together, and as of this writing, it remains aboard the lighthouse. In his basement shop back in Eastport, Howard Lewis carefully built nearly one hundred replacement balusters, which were painted and reinstalled. One of the kicked-out balusters was located in the water at Chesapeake Beach, Maryland, about fifteen miles southwest of Thomas Point. It was returned to the station and remains aboard. Just two weeks after the discovery of the vandal's damage, volunteers had completed cleaning and repairs and scheduled tours resumed.

By 2017, it was estimated that the lighthouse had received about $500,000 in renovations, but the demands of maintaining the lighthouse in a historically appropriate manner are insatiable. John Potvin, a longtime Chesapeake Bay sailor who can see the lighthouse from the backyard of his residence on Thomas Point Road, stepped up to lead the next phase of renovations. Potvin had recently retired from a career in property management and brought great passion to the project, along with a strong network of business and community contacts. By mid-2019, Potvin was serving as the preservation foreman for the next major phase of lighthouse preservation.

Above: Decorative balustrade on the lantern-level gallery. There are more than two hundred balusters on the six sides of the lighthouse. A number of them were damaged in a 2016 vandalism event. Howard Lewis, the great-grandson of a former keeper, built dozens of replacement balusters, to historical specs, in his Eastport woodshop. *Photo by the author.*

Right: John Potvin, a tireless volunteer at the Thomas Point Shoal Lighthouse, served as foreman of the extensive 2019 structural repair projects at the lighthouse. *Photo by the author.*

The painting and repairs of the exposed exterior of the cottage are an ongoing process. Fine Paints of Europe, a Vermont-based importer of Dutch paint with a long history of engagement with historic properties, has donated the paint for the projects. Scores of volunteers, including members of the Annapolis Woodworking Guild, spend days at the cottage scraping, painting and making repairs. About two-thirds of the cottage's wooden siding has been replaced since 2004. In 2019, a massive white oak beam, located directly beneath the outdoor privy and one of eight around the edge of the primary-level gallery, cracked. In keeping with the commitments to historic integrity, an appropriate replacement was sourced. The privy and railing were dismantled and stored inside the lighthouse. A scaffolding was built to allow access to the damaged beam. The replacement beam was in place and the privy and railing back in place by the end of November 2019.

By mid-2019, the cottage was receiving great attention, and the underwater structure was holding up well, but the condition of the metal between the

In October 2019, a temporary scaffolding was built on the southwest side of Thomas Point Shoal Lighthouse to allow workers to access a cracked beam beneath of the outdoor privy. *Photo by the author.*

cottage and the underwater structure kept John Potvin awake at night. The underwater structure, including the original nine wrought-iron screwpiles, is in place. Potvin explained, "The underwater structure is in perfect shape. We've had divers go all the way down to the bottom and inspect it and test it and it is as good today as it was in 1875."

However, none of the exposed steel beams running at water level between the screwpiles is original, and they were subject to frequent washings and even complete submersion in the Bay. These beams now showed various degrees of deterioration. The beams installed by the Coast Guard in the early 1990s seemed to be faring the worst. Complicating matters were the tie rods connecting the beams to the cottage. These had been replaced in 1980 and were also showing major deterioration. By 2019, multiple beams and tie rods needed to be replaced, and upon closer inspection, the situation seemed urgent.

To support this project, the Maryland Historic Trust again delivered a generous grant, as did other private organizations, including the Davidsonville (Maryland) Ruritan Club, the United States Lighthouse Society and the Chesapeake chapter of the United States Lighthouse Society. Simultaneously, John Potvin set to work generating publicity and additional funding for the effort. He escorted reporters and photographers to the lighthouse and patiently explained the history and the current

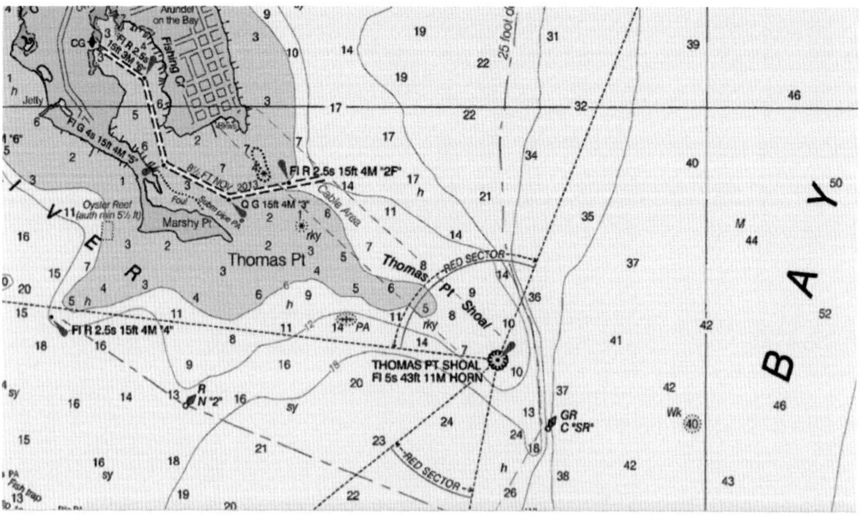

A 2019 chart of the Thomas Point Shoal. Note the dredged channel into Fishing Creek, ending at the present-day Coast Guard station. Remnants of the washed away point are marked on the chart. *Detail of NOAA Chart 122270 https://www.charts.noaa.gov.*

situation. He established an Internet fundraising page with a goal of raising $50,000 toward the project.

In early November 2019, as work began on the latest round of restoration, the United States Lighthouse Society and scores of volunteers organized a fundraising event for the Thomas Point preservation effort. More than two hundred guests gathered in a banquet hall at the United States Naval Academy stadium to celebrate the work at the lighthouse and raise additional funds for ongoing projects. John Potvin kicked off the evening by presenting Henry Gonzalez and the U.S. Lighthouse Society with a check for $20,000, contributed by an anonymous donor. Beyond that donation, an additional $34,000 was raised at the event.

Despite some weather challenges, the four most worrisome steel beams, six tie rods and the wooden oak beam were replaced within the next few weeks. Nearly 150 years after its commissioning, the work at the Thomas Point Shoal Lighthouse continues. It will never stop.

The original purpose of Thomas Point Shoal Lighthouse is clear. Its history, while colorful, is straightforward and linear. But everyone who sees or visits the screwpile in the twenty-first century feels something different. An unlikely structure connected to the same bit of earth for nearly 150 years elicits a range of reactions.

After Virginia Woolf made a lighthouse the central image of one of her most popular books, she explained the symbolism: "I saw that all sorts of feelings would accrue to this, trusted that people would make it the deposit for their own emotions—which they have done, one thinking it means one thing [and] another another."

To some, the Thomas Point Shoal Lighthouse is a powerful symbol. To others, it is a historic treasure evocative of a simpler time. To others still, it honors generations of service and sacrifice. The physical structure of the screwpile is seen as a challenging restoration project, a busy fishing spot and a backdrop to photos. In its own magical way, the lighthouse is all of these things and more, at the same time.

Over the course of its existence, the Thomas Point Shoal Lighthouse has seen more than fifty thousand high tides and countless storms. It has outlasted twenty-seven presidents and witnessed twenty-five thousand sunsets. Flipping calendar pages backward and forward from the day it was first lit, the day George Washington was born was closer to its opening than we are today.

Thomas Point Shoal Lighthouse at sunrise, September 2019. *Photo by the author.*

For nearly 150 years, across swaths of three centuries, this lighthouse has served and is served. The lighthouse has been damaged by ice, assaulted by hurricanes, threatened with dismantling on multiple occasions, vandalized and declared "excess to the needs of the United States of America." It has survived.

The lighthouse is undeniable.

SCREWPILES ON THE CHESAPEAKE

Forty-two screwpile lighthouses were built on the Chesapeake Bay. While some of these were damaged or destroyed by ice, the vast majority were disassembled or burned and replaced by beacons or caisson-style lighthouses. Only four of the Chesapeake's screwpile lighthouses remain standing, and only one of those, Thomas Point Shoal Lighthouse, is at its original location.

Seventeen Maryland lighthouses are among the more than 1,500 properties and districts located in Maryland in the National Register of Historic Places, including all four of its surviving screwpile lighthouses:

THOMAS POINT SHOAL LIGHTHOUSE. Located just south of Annapolis, Maryland. It was first lit in 1875, automated in 1986, listed in the National Register of Historic Places in 1975, designated as a National Historic Landmark in 1999 and transferred from the federal government to the City of Annapolis and its partners in 2004.

SEVEN FOOT KNOLL LIGHTHOUSE. Originally located at the mouth of the Patapsco River, now in Baltimore's Inner Harbor. Seven Foot Knoll was the first screwpile built on the Chesapeake and was first lit in 1856. The exterior of the house is covered by cast-iron plates. The lighthouse was automated in 1949 and replaced by a nearby beacon. In 1987, the lighthouse, in disrepair, was donated to the City of Baltimore by the United States Coast Guard. The structure was moved to Baltimore's Inner Harbor in 1988 and listed in the

Left: Sunrise at Thomas Point Shoal Lighthouse in September 2019 as workers prepare to replace a cracked wooden beam beneath the outdoor privy. *Photo by the author.*

Below: Seven Foot Knoll Light was the first screwpile built on the Chesapeake (1856). It was automated in 1949 and moved ashore at Baltimore's Inner Harbor in 1988. *Photo by Carol M. Highsmith, Library of Congress.*

National Register of Historic Places in 1989. Seven Foot Knoll is managed and preserved by Historic Ships in Baltimore and the Living Classrooms Foundation. The unique lighthouse is open to the public.

HOOPER STRAIT LIGHTHOUSE. Originally located at the entrance to Tangier Sound, in Dorchester County, on Maryland's Eastern Shore. Now located at the Chesapeake Bay Maritime Museum in St. Michaels, Maryland, it was the second screwpile built at the entrance to Tangier Sound. The first, lit in 1867, was destroyed in the 1877 ice event. The second screwpile at the site was built and lit in 1879. The lighthouse was automated in 1954, and the house was closed. In 1966, the Coast Guard decided to dismantle the structure, but the newly created Chesapeake Bay Maritime Museum, working with the Talbot Historical Society, stepped in to prevent the demolition. The federal government contributed the $14,000 it had budgeted for demolition. The lighthouse was cut in half and lifted from its foundation. Both halves were moved, via barge, sixty miles to St. Michaels, where they were reconnected atop a new base in November 1966. The Hooper Strait Lighthouse is a cornerstone of the Chesapeake Bay Maritime Museum's campus and is open to the public.

The Hooper Strait Lighthouse was built in 1879 and automated in 1964. It was moved to the Chesapeake Bay Maritime Museum in St. Michaels, Maryland, in 1966. The preservation of the Hooper Strait screwpile served as a model and inspiration for those who stepped forward to preserve Thomas Point in the 1970s. *Photo by Carol M. Highsmith, Library of Congress.*

DRUM POINT LIGHTHOUSE. Originally located at the mouth of the Patuxent River. It is now located at the Calvert Marine Museum in Solomons, Maryland. It was first lit in 1883, automated in 1960 and discontinued in 1962. In 1975, the Calvert County Historical Society, with the great assistance from a contractor who was building a nearby bridge over the Patuxent River, moved the structure to Solomons, Maryland. The Drum Point screwpile is on the grounds of the Calvert Marine Museum and is open to the public.

LIGHTHOUSES ON THE NATIONAL HISTORIC LANDMARK LIST

About 3 percent of the places listed in the National Register are also recognized as National Historic Landmarks, and only twelve American lighthouses are recognized in this fashion. Thomas Point Shoal Lighthouse is the only screwpile lighthouse receiving this recognition and the only Maryland lighthouse.

NATIONAL HISTORIC LANDMARK LIGHTHOUSES
Block Island Southeast Light, Rhode Island
Boston Light, Massachusetts
Cape Ann Light Station, Massachusetts
Cape Hatteras Lighthouse, North Carolina
Cape Henry Lighthouse, Virginia
Grosse Point Light, Illinois

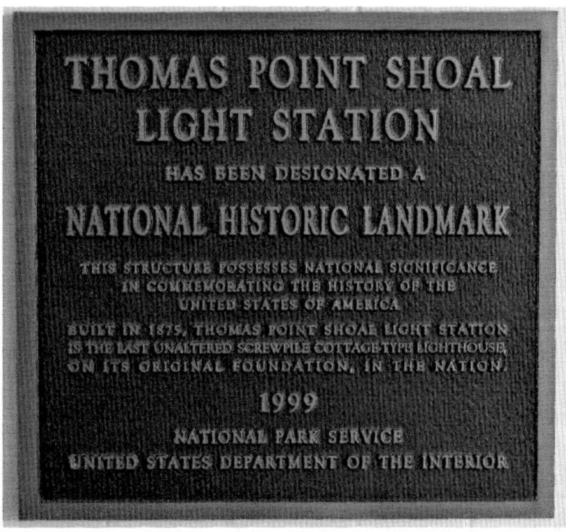

Plaque aboard the Thomas Point Shoal Lighthouse. Thomas Point is one of only twelve lighthouses in the United States to receive this recognition. *Photo by the author.*

Montauk Point Light, New York
Navesink Twin Lights, New Jersey
Ponce de Leon Inlet Light, Florida
Sandy Hook Light, New Jersey
Split Rock Lighthouse, Minnesota
Thomas Point Shoal Lighthouse, Maryland

THOMAS POINT TIMELINE

950–1600 Native Americans gather on the peninsula that would later be called Thomas Point, as verified by the presence of oyster shell middens found at the point.

1608 John Smith and crew make their first exploration of the Chesapeake Bay. They are likely the first Europeans to see the point.

1665 Philip Thomas receives a grant for 120 acres of land between the South and Severn Rivers at Annapolis, including the peninsula that would soon become known as "Thomas's Point."

1780 Baltimore is designated as an official port of entry.

1789 The United States Lighthouse Establishment is created and operates under the Department of the Treasury.

1792 The Cape Henry Lighthouse (Virginia) is the first lighthouse built by the United States Lighthouse Establishment.

1813 A British sloop is grounded on Thomas Point.

1822 French physicist Augustin Fresnel designs the Fresnel lens.

1823 Maryland's first lighthouse, a stone tower at Bodkin Island, near the mouth of the Patapsco River, is first lit.

1823 William Bedford Barney, the naval officer for the Port of Baltimore, officially requests a light at Thomas Point.

1824 Congress appropriates $6,500 for a lighthouse at Thomas Point. Jeremiah Chase sells land at Thomas Point to the federal government for $529.69 for the purpose of a lighthouse.

1825 The first Thomas Point Shore tower is lit.

1827 The Baltimore and Ohio Railroad Company is founded.

1828 On July 4, ninety-one-year-old Charles Carroll, a signer of the Declaration of Independence, turns the earth with a spade and ceremoniously begins construction of the Baltimore and Ohio Railroad.

1830 Baltimore becomes the second-most populated city in the United States.

1840 The rebuilt (second) Thomas Point Shore tower is first lit.

1841 Alexander Mitchell's River Thames screwpile is first lit.

1841 A Fresnel lens is installed on the Navesink Lighthouse in New Jersey, at the entrance to the New York Narrows, the first instance of its use in the United States.

1845 The United States Naval Academy is founded in Annapolis, Maryland, about five and a half miles northwest of Thomas Point.

1850 America's first screwpile lighthouse is opened at Brandywine Shoal, Delaware Bay.

1851 The U.S. Lighthouse Board takes over from the U.S. Lighthouse Establishment and operates under the Treasury Department.

1852 The Baltimore and Ohio Railroad reaches the Ohio River, 379 miles from Baltimore.

1855 A new Fifth Order Fresnel lens is installed at the Thomas Point tower.

1865 President Abraham Lincoln is slowed by ice off Thomas Point en route by steamer to a peace conference in the lower Chesapeake Bay.

1868 Over the course of the year, ten thousand immigrants pass Thomas Point on their way to Baltimore.

1871 Duxbury Pier Light (Massachusetts) is the first caisson lighthouse to be built in the United States.

1873 Congress appropriates $20,000 to build a new screwpile lighthouse at the end of the Thomas Point Shoal.

1874 The State of Maryland transfers ownership of a plot of Chesapeake Bay bottom at the end of the Thomas Point Shoal to the federal government for the purpose of building a new lighthouse.

1875 The Baltimore and Ohio Railroad reaches Chicago, 811 miles from Baltimore.

1875 Congress approves an additional $15,000 "for completing" the screwpile lighthouse at Thomas Point. The new Thomas Point Shoal Lighthouse is lit for the first time on November 20, 1875. It shows a 3½ Order Fresnel lens.

1877 Kerosene becomes the primary fuel for lighthouses.

1877 Ice floes damage the Thomas Point Shoal Lighthouse and force a brief abandonment of the station. A replacement Fourth Order Fresnel lens is installed.

1882 More than forty-two thousand immigrants arrive at the Port of Baltimore via ship.

1886 More than 1,400 cubic yards of stone are placed around the Thomas Point Shoal Lighthouse foundation to further protect it from ice.

1886 The Statue of Liberty is the first lighthouse to use electricity. (The statue was, in its early years, officially part of the United States lighthouse network.)

1896 The second tower at Thomas Point collapses. Anything remaining of value at the point is sold at auction and removed.

1899 A replacement Fourth Order fixed Fresnel lens is installed at Thomas Point Shoal Lighthouse.

1903 The U.S. Lighthouse Board moves from the Treasury Department to the new Department of Commerce.

1903 Thomas Point Shoal Lighthouse assistant keeper Henry Addicks mysteriously disappears from the station.

1910 The United States Lighthouse Board disbands, and a new Lighthouse Service is created, under the Department of Commerce.

1912 Thomas Point Shoal Lighthouse beacon changes from "Flash every thirty seconds" to "Flash every five seconds." The Lighthouse Service makes the change to "conform to modern methods of lighting and give increased efficiency."

1914 An island at the tip of Thomas Point, once the site of the shore towers, is sold to a private party by the federal government.

1919 The United States Lighthouse Board undertakes an $1,800 project at the Thomas Point Shoal Lighthouse to "[r]estore light station to original strength."

1933 In August, the Chesapeake and Potomac Hurricane washes nearly a ton of coal away from its storage bin located on the Thomas Point Shoal Lighthouse lower platform.

1934 Thomas Point Shoal Lighthouse is electrified via generators.

1939 The Commerce Department's Lighthouse Service is merged into the United States Coast Guard.

1952–53 New ten-thousand-foot electrical cable is run from shore to the Thomas Point Shoal Lighthouse and then connected on shore to commercial power source.

1972 The U.S. Coast Guard considers decommissioning the lighthouse and dismantling the Thomas Point Shoal Lighthouse cottage. The public rallies around the lighthouse, and the decision is delayed.

1972 Coast Guard Station Annapolis is opened on Thomas Point Road at Fishing Creek, about two miles from the Thomas Point Shoal Lighthouse.

1975 Thomas Point Shoal Lighthouse is listed in the National Register of Historic Places.

1975 Thomas Point Shoal Lighthouse's centennial is celebrated with Coast Guardsman John White in command at the station. White is the station's first black keeper.

1980 The Coast Guard announces that the Thomas Point Shoal Lighthouse will be automated and begins search for a civilian caretaker.

1986 Thomas Point Shoal Lighthouse is automated but remains in the care of the federal government. The station's Fresnel lens is removed and taken to safekeeping in Coast Guard offices at Curtis Bay, Maryland, near Baltimore.

1997 Thomas Point Shoal Lighthouse is converted to solar and battery power.

1999 Thomas Point Shoal Lighthouse is designated as a National Historic Landmark, one of only twelve American lighthouses to receive such a designation.

2000 The National Lighthouse Preservation Act of 2000 includes a concept designed to facilitate the transfer of historic lighthouses to well-vetted local governments and nonprofit organizations.

2002 In conjunction with the U.S. Coast Guard, the federal government's General Services Administration declares the Thomas Point Shoal Lighthouse "excess to the needs of the United States of America." The Thomas Point Shoal Lighthouse is listed as available for transfer.

2003 The City of Annapolis partners with the United States Lighthouse Society, the Annapolis Maritime Museum and Anne Arundel County to apply for ownership of the Thomas Point Shoal Lighthouse.

2004 The Thomas Point Shoal Lighthouse transfer ceremony conveys the lighthouse from the United States Coast Guard to the City of Annapolis. The United States Lighthouse Society is granted a long-term lease from the city to manage and preserve the Thomas Point Shoal Lighthouse, supported by the Annapolis Maritime Museum and Anne Arundel County.

2005 Volunteers, many from the Chesapeake chapter of the U.S. Lighthouse Society, begin ongoing preservation efforts at the Thomas Point Shoal Lighthouse.

2007 More than six hundred guests visit the Thomas Point Shoal Lighthouse as part of tours run by the Annapolis Maritime Museum.

2016 Vandals board the Thomas Point Shoal Lighthouse, break windows and damage the cottage.

2019 Major fundraising efforts are launched to restore the steel structure supporting the Thomas Point Shoal Lighthouse. Repairs are underway by the end of the year.

BIBLIOGRAPHY

Annual Report of the Light-House Board of the United States to the Secretary of the Treasury. July 7, 1852. Library of Congress, https://lccn.loc.gov/09035241.

The Arundel-on-the-Bay History Project. *The Amazing Story of Arundel-On-The-Bay*. Arundel-on-the-Bay, MD: self-published, 2018.

Baker, Ira Osborn. *A Treatise on Masonry Construction.* New York: J. Wiley & Sons, 1889.

De Gast, Robert. *The Lighthouses of the Chesapeake.* Baltimore, MD: Johns Hopkins University Press, 1973.

Eshelman, Ralph E., and Burton K. Kummerow. *In Full Glory Reflected: Discovering the War of 1812 in the Chesapeake Bay.* Baltimore: Maryland Historical Society Press and the Maryland Historic Trust Press, 2012.

Gaugard, Jules. "Foundations." *Van Nostrand's Engineering Magazine* 18 (January–June 1878).

Harper's Weekly. "Poached Oysters." March 1, 1884.

Healey, David. *Great Storms of the Chesapeake.* Charleston, SC: The History Press, 2012.

Ingram, J.S. *The Centennial Exposition, Described and Illustrated.* Philadelphia, PA: Hubbard Bros., 1876.

Marin, David. "A Guiding Light." *Coast Guard Mid-Atlantic*, official blog of the Fifth Coast Guard District, October 9, 2015.

National Historic Landmark Nomination. Prepared by Ralph Eshelman and edited by Candace Clifford, NCSHPO consultant. U.S. Lighthouse Society Cooperative Agreement with the National Park Service's National Maritime Initiative, 1996.

National Register of Historic Places Nomination Form. Prepared by the United States Coast Guard, 1975.

Putnam, George R. *Lighthouses and Light Ships of the United States.* Boston, MA: Houghton Mifflin, 1917.

Report of the United States Light-House Board, September 1, 1876. United States Congressional Serial Set, vol. 1752. https://hdl.handle.net/2027/uc1.b3985820.

Tag, Thomas. "Lighthouse Lamps through Time." U.S. Lighthouse Society. https://uslhs.org.

United States Light-House Establishment. *Instructions to Light-Keepers, July 1881.* Washington, D.C.: Government Printing Office, 1881.

United States Lighthouse Society. "Thomas Point Shoal Lighthouse." https://uslhs.org.

United States Lighthouse Society, Chesapeake chapter. https://cheslights.org.

———. Workday logs from the Thomas Point Shoal Lighthouse. https://cheslights.org.

United States Senate. *Senate Documents*, vol. 171. Washington, D.C.: Government Printing Office, 1862.

Vojetch, Pat. *Lighting the Bay.* Centreville, MD: Tidewater Publishers, 1996.

Wakelyn, Jon L. *Birth of the Bill of Rights: Biographies.* Westport, CT: Greenwood Press, 2004.

Wennersten, John R. *The Oyster Wars of Chesapeake Bay.* Centreville, MD: Tidewater Publishers, 1981.

Whedbee, T. Courtenay J. *The Port of Baltimore in the Making, 1828–1878.* Baltimore, MD: privately printed, 1953.

YouTube. "Four Rivers Heritage Area—Bob Stevenson Thomas Point Shoal Lighthouse EXTENDED." https://www.youtube.com.

Newspapers

Annapolis Maryland Republican and State Capital Advertiser.

Baltimore Sun.

The Capital (Annapolis).

Cumberland (MD) Evening Times.

Evening Capital (Annapolis).

Maryland Gazette.

New York Herald.

INDEX

A

B

C

D

E

F

G

H

J

K

L

U

V

W

Y

ABOUT THE AUTHOR

A lifelong Chesapeake Bay sailor, David Gendell is the cofounder of *SpinSheet*, the Annapolis-based Chesapeake Bay sailing magazine. He is a U.S. Coast Guard–licensed captain, an accomplished racing sailor and an aspiring fisherman. He is a distinguished alumni of St. Mary's High School in Annapolis and, between sailing adventures, graduated from Randolph-Macon College in Ashland, Virginia. In 2004, he was the emcee of the transfer ceremony that shifted ownership of the Thomas Point Shoal Lighthouse from the federal government to the City of Annapolis and its partners. He lives in Annapolis with his family.